'Too many manuals mistake best practice for the mastery of techniques and so relegate the role of values to a perfunctory preface. *Values-Based Practice*, however, re-opens the door to another view, in which values are at the core of our being and doing – "the blood that courses through our veins" – for all critical and ethical practitioners addressing the impact of complex forms of oppression in the lives of the people they work with and for.'

Dr Phillip Ablett, *Queensland University of Technology, Australia*

'Students and practitioners in a range of settings will benefit from the fresh light this thought-provoking manual throws on the nature and importance of values in "people work". Easy to read and full of opportunities for the reader to reflect on their own journey into practice, to see more clearly "who they are", it will provide readers with an invaluable anchor point for professional practice and for decision making in the future.'

Iolo Madoc Jones, *Professor of Criminal and Social Justice, Wrexham University*

'In this updated manual, Thompson and Moss present the centrality of values in working with people, bringing together and developing a range of pertinent ideas. They usefully introduce key concepts and offer ideas for reflection and development in a coherent flow. I enjoyed going through this edition, as it enabled me to look in a mirror at whether I can be part of the solution, rather than part of the problem. It offers an invaluable resource for people ranging from students to experienced practitioners in remembering the important core underpinning our work.'

Abyd Quinn Aziz, *Reader in Social Work, Qualified Social Worker and Board Member, Social Care Wales*

Values-Based Practice

This second edition of *Values-Based Practice* aids readers to understand the key role of values as a basis for effective practice across human services and beyond. Neglecting values when working with vulnerable people can lead to disastrous and unethical outcomes. However, the concept of values can be difficult to grasp.

The authors combat this difficulty by fusing theoretical understanding with helpful practice guidance to clearly demonstrate how to keep values at the centre of good practice. Key concepts are provided and ideas for reflection offered to encourage the importance of understanding values in practice.

An invaluable resource for practitioners and students across the human services, including education, health, social work and social care, youth work, counselling, pastoral and police, as well as probation professionals and managers across all sectors.

Neil Thompson is a well-known and highly respected author in social work and the human relations field more broadly. He is currently a visiting professor at The Open University and Wrexham University. His online platform, The Neil Thompson Academy, offers a range of learning opportunities, including leadership qualifications.

Bernard Moss was Emeritus Professor of Social Work Education and Spirituality at Staffordshire University, where he began working with social work students in 1993. His particular teaching interests focused on communication skills, studies in death, dying and bereavement, and mediation studies.

Practice Manuals for Busy Professionals

Managing Stress, 2nd edition
Neil Thompson

Effective Problem Solving, 2nd edition
Neil Thompson

Crisis Intervention, 3rd edition
Neil Thompson

Care of Older People: A Values Perspective, 2nd edition
Sue Thompson

Spirituality and Religion in Human Services: A Guide for Practitioners and Managers, 2nd edition
Neil Thompson and Bernard Moss

Anti-Racist Practice, 2nd edition
Neil Thompson

Values-Based Practice: A Guide for Practitioners and Managers, 2nd edition
Neil Thompson and Bernard Moss

Values-Based Practice

A Guide for Practitioners and Managers

Second Edition

Neil Thompson and Bernard Moss

With a Foreword by Professor Harry Ferguson

Routledge
Taylor & Francis Group

LONDON AND NEW YORK

Designed cover image: Getty Images

Second edition published 2026
by Routledge
4 Park Square, Milton Park, Abingdon, Oxon, OX14 4RN

and by Routledge
605 Third Avenue, New York, NY 10158

Routledge is an imprint of the Taylor & Francis Group, an informa business

For Product Safety Concerns and Information please contact our EU representative
GPSR@taylorandfrancis.com. Taylor & Francis Verlag GmbH, Kaufingerstraße 24,
80331 München, Germany.

First edition published in 2022 by Avenue Media Solutions.

British Library Cataloguing-in-Publication Data
A catalogue record for this book is available from the British Library

ISBN: 978-1-041-17199-7 (hbk)
ISBN: 978-1-041-17424-0 (pbk)
ISBN: 978-1-003-68961-4 (ebk)

DOI: 10.4324/9781003689614

Typeset in Times New Roman
by Newgen Publishing UK

Contents

Welcome!   xii
About the authors   xiii
Acknowledgements   xiv
Preface to the second edition   xv
Foreword by Harry Ferguson   xvii

Introduction   1
Why a manual?   3
How do I use it?   3

1 What's this got to do with me?   5
Introduction   5
The importance of values   5
What do values do?   7
Introducing the values debate   9
Self-awareness   13
Conclusion   18

2 Making sense of values   20
Introduction   20
The values debate   21
An overview of the values debate   24

CONTENTS

	Taking a wider view	27
	Political correctness (PC)	33
	A note on being 'woke'	35
	Promoting equality	36
	A note on equality	38
	Anti-discriminatory practice	39
	Values-based practice	41
	Conclusion	42
3	**Confidentiality**	**43**
	Introduction	43
	Why is confidentiality important?	43
	What is confidentiality?	44
	Boundaries	45
	Guidelines for good practice	48
	Conclusion	50
4	**Tackling discrimination and oppression**	**52**
	Introduction	52
	The struggle for social justice	52
	Celebrating diversity	53
	Countering discrimination and oppression: Some examples from practice	56
	Countering discrimination and oppression: Religious and spiritual issues	60
	Reflective practice	61
	Reflexive practice	62
	Conclusion	63
5	**Working in partnership**	**65**
	Introduction	65
	Some examples from practice	67
	Working positively with tensions and conflicts	69
	Wider community networks	70
	An example from practice: Faith communities	71
	Conclusion	72
6	**Rights and choice**	**73**
	Introduction	73
	Why are rights and choice important?	73
	What are rights?	73
	Clients have a right to ...	74
	The significance of choice	78
	When should rights and choice be overridden?	78
	Conclusion	79

7 Individuality and identity   **80**
Introduction   *80*
Why are individuality and identity important?   *80*
What are individuality and identity?   *80*
Personal beliefs   *81*
Knowing and assuming   *83*
Guidelines for good practice   *84*
Conclusion   *85*

8 Valuing diversity   **87**
Introduction   *87*
What is diversity?   *87*
Some examples from practice   *89*
A framework for evaluating various value systems   *90*
Class and religion   *90*
Conclusion   *91*

9 Values at work   **93**
Introduction   *93*
Why work matters   *93*
Values in the workplace   *94*
Value conflicts   *96*
Exploitation or partnership?   *98*
Workplace health and wellbeing   *99*
The importance of leadership   *100*
Conclusion   *101*

10 Practising ethically   **102**
Introduction   *102*
Exploring some codes of practice   *103*
Comments on these codes   *105*
Power: Social work as a case example   *106*
Implications for other professionals   *108*
Challenging inequality   *109*

11 Promoting recovery   **112**
Introduction   *112*
Why mental health? Why recovery?   *112*
Recovery: An example from practice   *114*
Acknowledging risk   *115*
Hope   *116*
Conclusion   *117*

CONTENTS

12 Identifying people's needs and strengths **118**
Introduction *118*
Resilience *120*
Spirituality *121*
Supporting a variety of lifestyles *122*
Conclusion *123*

13 Providing person-centred care **124**
Introduction *124*
An example from practice *125*
The importance of evaluation *127*
Conclusion *128*

14 Making a difference **129**
Introduction *129*
Achieving the highest standards *129*
Exploring our vulnerability *130*
Spiritual intelligence: SQ *132*
Conclusion *134*

15 Promoting safety and positive risk taking **136**
Introduction *136*
Some living examples *136*
Problems with defining risk *138*
Conclusion *140*

16 Values today and tomorrow **141**
Introduction *141*
The changing world of work *142*
Neoliberalism and beyond *143*
The future of democracy *144*
Religion and spirituality *145*
Values and the media *147*
Environmental challenges *147*
The wellbeing economy *148*
Conclusion *148*

17 Conclusion **150**

Guide to further learning **152**
Books and academic journals *152*
Research and reports *152*
Online resources and websites *153*

Training resources	*153*
Key research articles and theories	*154*
Professional organizations and associations	*154*
References	**155**

Welcome!

... to this practice manual on values-based practice. Many people make the mistake of thinking that values are abstract things unconnected with the reality of their day-to-day lives. Nothing could be further from the truth. Everything we do is touched in some way by our values, by those principles and beliefs that we hold dear.

This manual has been developed to help you appreciate just how significant values are in shaping our work and, indeed, our lives more broadly. The more 'tuned in' we are to our values, the more we can draw on them as a source of motivation, sustenance and resilience.

Written by two highly experienced and well-respected authors with many years' experience in practice, this manual should not only give you plenty of food for thought, but also help you develop the quality of your practice in whatever branch of the people professions you work.

About the authors

Neil Thompson is an independent writer, educator and adviser. He has held full or honorary professorships at five UK universities and has been a speaker at seminars and conferences in the UK, Ireland, Italy, Spain, Portugal, Greece, the Netherlands, Norway, the Czech Republic, Turkey, Hong Kong, India, Canada, the USA and Australia. He is also a visiting professor at the Open University. He now runs the Neil Thompson Academy, providers of online learning resources, including Chartered Management Institute qualifications. His website, with his acclaimed *Manifesto for Making a Difference*, is at www.NeilThompson.info.

Bernard Moss was Emeritus Professor of Social Work Education and Spirituality at Staffordshire University, where he began working with social work students in 1993. His particular teaching interests focused on communication skills, studies in death, dying and bereavement, and mediation studies. He was formerly Director of the Centre for Spirituality and Health at Staffordshire University, and made significant contributions to debates on this important theme. In 2004 he was awarded a National Teaching Fellowship by the Higher Education Academy to mark his teaching excellence, and he became a Senior Fellow in 2007. He was a founding member of the British Association for the Study of Spirituality (now the International Network for the Study of Spirituality). Bernard's earlier career included roles as a probation officer, relationship counsellor, mediator and leader of a faith community. He passed away while the first edition of this manual was being finalized prior to going to press.

Acknowledgements

We would both like to thank the various students and practitioners we have worked with over the years who have helped us broaden and deepen our understanding of the role values play in professional practice and beyond.

We would also like to thank Geoffrey Mann of Russell House publishing who generously allowed us to use materials previously published in the *Theory into Practice* series of books. Geoffrey turned out to be a good friend as well as a good colleague.

Thanks also go to our respective partners, Sue and Sheila, who have been such towers of strength over many years. We are also grateful to Anna Thompson for her sterling editorial work in bringing about the publication of this work.

Finally, we would like to thank Professor Harry Ferguson for his very supportive Foreword.

Preface to the second edition

I first met Bernard Moss over 30 years ago and was immediately impressed not only by his extensive knowledge base and his great skill in teaching students so effectively and inspirationally about the subject matter, but also his warmth, sincerity, generosity of spirit and sheer humanity. Straight away I knew I wanted this man to be a good friend and, thankfully, that is what happened. His passing away, just as the text for the first edition of this manual was being finalized, was therefore a great tragedy, not only for me, but also for everyone who had benefited from his wisdom, his perceptive insights and the very special qualities he brought.

Thankfully, we had discussed the plans for the manual to such an extent that I was able to add the finishing touches in a way that I knew he would have approved of, consistent with his approach and his beliefs. Likewise, I have been able to develop the second edition in keeping with his views and perspectives, although that has not proven at all difficult as we were very much 'on the same page'.

This manual has grown out of two previous publications. First, Bernard and I co-wrote open learning resources on the value base of social care. Subsequently, Bernard wrote a book, simply entitled *Values*, that appeared in a series of books on theory and practice for which I was the series editor. Once both of these were out of print, I proposed to Bernard that we combine, extend and update the materials to offer a modern-day resource to help students, practitioners and managers learn about the importance of values-based practice. Bernard welcomed my suggestion and particularly liked the idea of it being in the form of a practice manual. So, while the manual contains a lot of very helpful theoretical material, its main focus is on practice.

It is a great tragedy that readers of this manual will never get the opportunity to be exposed to Bernard's inspirational teaching and experience his profound humanity directly. The excellent insights offered in this manual are the closest we can now get.

For this revised and updated edition, I have maintained the original materials, added additional comments in places and taken the opportunity to incorporate consideration of wider developments that have occurred since writing the first edition. The overall message, however, remains the same: values are at the heart of everything we do; the greater our understanding of values, the better equipped we will be to rise to the challenges we face, whether in the workplace or in our private lives.

Dr Neil Thompson

Foreword

The aim of this manual is to inform, educate, challenge and inspire those who work in the human services, such as doctors, nurses, midwives, occupational therapists, podiatrists, mental health nurses, social workers, social care workers, probation officers, police and prison officers, counsellors, youth and community workers, advice workers, and staff in faith-based organizations. Producing a text that can have relevance to such a wide audience is a bold undertaking, for it involves drawing out the core values that underpin helping and illustrating what it is to be helpful. But, as it shows, what it means to be helpful is far from straightforward, as it is infused with complex dilemmas about the uses of power and care and control. Above all, the manual helps professionals practise in anti-discriminatory and anti-oppressive ways by exploring the nature and implications of a values-based approach. Bernard Moss and Neil Thompson argue that particular kinds of values need to be at the heart of the helping professions based on treating people equally, protecting human rights and promoting diversity, all through placing relationships, person-centred care, partnership working, carefully assessed risk-taking and critically reflective practice centre stage.

While it takes theory seriously, the manual avoids lengthy intellectual argument for its own sake. Academic texts that deal with the ethical dimensions of practice tend to prescribe in abstract ways what practitioners should do to work in ethical ways. This manual is a strategic attempt to go beyond wishful thinking to ground values in day-to-day working realities. Many useful examples are offered. As the authors point out, while helping vulnerable people can be incredibly rewarding, it is also often stressful, emotionally demanding and carried out in organizational contexts where resources are limited and the 'right' ways of being helpful are ideologically contested, all of which means that the value base of professionals can so easily be eroded by work pressures and anxieties. This manual provides an invaluable resource for practitioners' and managers' learning and ethical development, but also one they can come back to when they need to renew themselves and their skills and commitment to values-based practice.

In achieving this, the manual focuses on a wide range of factors that shape our values, including gender, age, race, ethnicity, abilities, sexualities, social class. Particularly welcome is the too often neglected influence of spirituality (in its widest sense) and what brings meaning to everyday life. The manual is infused with a moral urgency and commitment to help readers become 'the best practitioner you can be', insisting on honest engagement by the reader with what the implications are for their own practice, their own professional selves and development. The authors prove themselves to be reliable and trustworthy guides on this journey because of how they are prepared to model the kind of personal engagement and development it takes to become a values-based practitioner. Between them they brought to this manual an extraordinary amount of relevant experience, estimating that over the years they have run as many as 2,000 training courses for human service professionals. Teachers learn from those they teach and that's an awful lot of learning from practitioners that, alongside impressive intellectual engagement, is put to excellent use here. A central argument of this manual is that professional values are deeply personal. We embody them, but they are not static. A powerful example of this is Neil's and Bernard's remarkably open and honest accounts of themselves and the formation of their own values. Bernard's ends:

> And I remember the times when, as a man, I have cried – sometimes in front of others – realising slowly that that was not something to be ashamed of, and that there are other, more authentic, patterns of masculinity than the macho bravura that often surrounded me.

This moving passage exemplifies the integrity and humanity that are at the heart of this manual. Neil writes movingly about losing his dear friend and collaborator towards the end of the process of producing this work. It is desperately sad that Bernard did not live to see it in print. There are pleasure and pain in the creative process but, undoubtedly a great joy of co-production is being able to share the pride and satisfaction that come with bringing a writing project such as this to completion, to life. Like Neil now has, Bernard would have had so much to be proud of the vital contribution *Values-Based Practice* makes to the human service professions.

Professor Harry Ferguson
University of Birmingham

Introduction

This manual has been written for anyone and everyone who is involved in working with people in the human services – or 'people work' as we prefer to call it – no matter what setting you may be in. If success in your line of work relies on how effectively you relate to people, then values will be playing a significant role, and this manual can help you understand what is involved.

We live in challenging times for professional people workers: structures, roles and expectations change quickly, and many of the organizations committed to people work are likely to change, possibly beyond all recognition, in the decade ahead. The world of work has become more challenging over time for a variety of reasons (Cheese, 2021), and so it is sadly the case that many people now struggle to find meaning and fulfilment in their work, with the result that low levels of engagement are now common (Gallup, 2024). This is highly problematic for employers and employees alike (we shall return to this point in Chapter 16). Drawing succour, motivation and determination from our values is therefore all the more important.

For some people, the major changes in the world of work are exciting and challenging; for others, they are daunting and bewildering; but for all of us there remains the most important task of all, that of ensuring that those who come to us for help and assistance – whether as clients or colleagues – receive the best possible service. As people workers, we exist to help make a difference to other people's lives, no matter what discipline or profession we have chosen to follow or what our role is as practitioner, manger or educator. And fundamental to all our practice is the key issues of values.

This manual explores the value base of people work and, in doing so, seeks to offer a fresh look at a topic that, for some of you, may seem like 'old hat', for there are some disciplines where much has already been written on this theme.

DOI: 10.4324/9781003689614-1

Nevertheless, the importance of this topic for all people workers cannot be stressed highly enough. Our value base can so easily be eroded by the pressures and anxieties of the work, and sometimes a fresh light thrown on a familiar picture from a different angle can help us reclaim and re-energize our commitment to best practice.

The manual involves exploring the theory base, but not for theory's sake – rather, for the sake of seeing how it can inform practice (Thompson, 2017). In so doing, we provide opportunities for you to reflect on your own journey as individuals and as professionals, and the impact that your own values have had upon you. Set within an overview of some of the key themes that are central to values-based practice are some exercises intended to help you polish your reflective mirrors in order to see yourselves more clearly. Throughout the manual it is argued that values permeate our lives as people workers. They are not like polish that we apply from a tin when wanting to give the car a gleaming finish. They are more akin to the blood that courses through our veins and affects how and who we are. Therefore, although the manual looks at the theory base, it also challenges you to think about how these issues have been absorbed into your own bloodstream as people workers.

A key element of the manual is the examination of discrimination and oppression, but instead of adopting an academic approach, we take further the challenge to you to explore the implications of a values-based *practice* approach. There are also key points and exercises to encourage you to reflect on the importance of values to your own professional practice, plus 'Reflective moments' where you are invited to look at issues from your own point of view, premised on the idea of genuine understanding of other people being based on appreciating the situation from their point of view.

We also offer a *Guide to further learning* with suggestions for further study, with recommendations for some key books and important websites worth exploring.

This manual should be seen as a first word, not the last word on the subject; it is (in quiz game parlance) your starter for ten. It is not a comprehensive reader that brings together key texts from the important literature on the subject, although it will give you pointers to some of the most helpful material to consult. Nor will it explore all the values implications of all aspects of professional practice – that would be far too ambitious, although again it will offer you some practice issues to consider.

Instead, the manual aims to:

- Introduce you to some of the key issues in the debate;
- Provide you with an opportunity to explore these issues in your own time and at your own pace; and
- Provide material that could be used in small group discussion as well as in individual study; and, most importantly, engage with you, and encourage you to work at this all-important set of issues that underpin practice.

It is, of course, entirely up to you how you use it. In preparing it, we were well aware of the pressures on students, practitioners and managers and that speed reading and selectively skimming the literature are important skills to develop. A practice manual, however, makes different demands upon readers. This is why we lay out below some guidelines, in the *How do I use it?* section, to help you get the best out of it.

This manual can only be a starter: it will have served its purpose well if it encourages you to go further and deeper on your own journey towards the goal of best practice. Travel well!

Why a manual?

The word 'manual' comes from the Latin word for hand (as in manual labour, manual dexterity and so on), so a manual is a *hand*book. By 'handbook' what we mean is a set of guidelines that can help in direct practice. It is not the sort of text you might scan through to look for a quote to include in an essay; it is a basis for practice. For students, this means that it is likely to be of more use to you on placement (or in preparing for placement) than in your academic work. For practitioners, it is likely to be of more use to you in reviewing and consolidating your practice than in pursuing any further or higher qualifications. It is about *making a difference*.

But don't confuse the idea of a handbook, in the sense that we are using it here, with a 'procedures manual' or set of instructions. Professional practice is far too complex to simply follow instructions. Each chapter provides food for thought and insights from our own extensive experience, plus what we have learned from being managers, consultants, expert witnesses and educators. We estimate that we have run something in the region of 2,000 training courses over the years, so that is an awful lot of conversations that we have been able to learn from, an awful lot of unofficial, informal research that has taught us what people struggle with, how things go wrong and, just as importantly, what works well. This manual is therefore a distillation of that learning.

Imagine the manual as a senior colleague whose experience and knowledge you can draw on to help and guide you, but not simply as someone who will tell you what to do or make your decisions for you.

How do I use it?

The best answer we can give is to use it in the way that works best for you. To work out what that might be, we suggest that you read it through from start to finish initially. It doesn't need to be an in-depth read, and would not include doing the exercises, but it should give you an overview of what the manual is about, and the nature of the project you will be embarking on when you are ready to start engaging with the material more fully.

It isn't necessary to work on the chapters in the order we've presented them in, but we recommend that you use the following four-stage approach to make the best use of the manual. These are only suggestions: this is your journey, no-one else's, and you need to decide how best to tackle it.

- *Stage one*: speed read the manual to gain an overview.
- *Stage two*: spend a lot of time on the chapter about 'locating yourself'. Until you know where you are, you cannot locate yourself on the map in order to begin the journey.
- *Stage three*: select individual chapters according to your interest, and work through them, following up particular issues in the suggested reading.
- *Stage four*: when you have completed the manual, keep it somewhere easily accessible and revisit it from time to time. The chances are that, as you look back on the responses you made first time through, you will want to modify them in the light of further thought and reflection. This is why the metaphor of the journey is so important: we all continue to explore the implications of this all-important aspect of becoming effective, values-based workers. The journey never ends.

When you work on it, and how much time you spend on it, are also entirely up to you. It is designed as an aid for your own reflection, a guide or companion for *your* learning journey, so use it in a way that works for you. It is *your* thinking space. Share your thoughts with others if you want to or keep your reflections private if you prefer. You might write down your thoughts as part of a process of thinking things through. Or you might want to jot down key points; or, if you've been inspired by the tips, to add some of your own or remind yourself of useful tips provided by others, or a combination of these and more.

We have only one request in relation to how you use it. If you are serious about developing into the best practitioner, manager or educator you can be, then don't skip the exercises and do make some notes that are personal to you and your circumstances. We'd like to think that the discussion sections provide useful and relevant general material on the topics explored but, if you don't move beyond that 'taking information in' stage to the 'what are the implications of this for my own practice?' stage, then you won't get the full benefit of this aid to learning. And that would be a shame for everyone, not least the people who, now or in the future, rely on your support. So, now to the first of those important, but often overlooked, things to remember about values-based practice.

What's this got to do with me?

Introduction

'An awful lot' is the short answer to the question in the title of this chapter. Let's look at this in more detail, so that we have clarity about just how significant values are. We begin by looking at why values are important in professional practice generally and then focus in particular on how they relate specifically to *you*, in your practice, just as they do to all of us in our practice.

The importance of values

Without an awareness of values, our practice can become dangerous

This strong statement sets the tone for this manual. It argues that an awareness of values, linked to an ability to work within a values framework, is of fundamental importance to anyone who works with people, particularly in a professional context. It is not an optional extra, but rather lies at the very heart of best practice, however that is to be defined. As Jowitt and O'Loughlin (2005) so aptly put it: 'Values ... are not only the heart of ... practice, but they constitute the life force that permeates every part of ... practice' (p. 7).

This book is therefore about 'people work' and is aimed at all those who are engaged with working with people in wide variety of agencies and settings. By people work we mean those occupations and professions that work with people on a daily basis, whereby they seek to help them to overcome difficulties, challenges and obstacles that may be preventing them living life to the full or are somehow

DOI: 10.4324/9781003689614-2

affecting their health, wellbeing or personal effectiveness. If you work with people in this way, this manual and the issues it raises are for you.

In line with Jowitt and O'Loughlin (2005), it is our claim in this manual that *values are not only the heart of people work practice, but they also constitute the life force that permeates every part of practice in the human services.* How we define values is important, of course. One attempt by Clark (2000) provides a useful framework for our discussions. He argues that

> values give expression to intuitions and beliefs about the essential ends of human life and social living. Basic values embrace the grand aspirations or big ideas of morality and politics, such as freedom, justice, autonomy and community. Basic values also comprise ideals about the morally good character and the nature of life worth living, for example compassion, courage, truthfulness and industriousness.
>
> (p. 28, cited in Parker, 2004, p. 4)

How this works out in practice across a range of professions is the topic of this manual. You will find more detailed discussion of values from a philosophical point of view in various texts – see the *Guide to further learning* near the end of the manual.

The manual is aimed at a multi-professional readership and seeks to be a general introduction to key themes and issues for anyone who is studying to enter a career in any branch of people work. This includes the broad range of health professionals (doctors, nurses, midwives, occupational therapists, podiatrists, mental health nurses and so on); as well as social workers, social care workers, probation officers, police and prison officers, counsellors, youth and community workers, and the increasingly important 'army' of advice workers who not only staff the nationwide Citizens Advice network, but are also being employed by local authorities and a large number of agencies in the voluntary and private sectors to ensure that people know about, and then claim, the benefits to which they are entitled. The issues are also deeply relevant to those training for leadership roles in faith-based organizations and, indeed, as we mentioned earlier, anyone where success in your work depends on how you relate to *people*, including managers, leaders and HR professionals across all sectors.

This multi-professional approach is particularly important in the twenty-first century. One of the characteristic features of twentieth-century 'people work' was the way in which various professionals worked in parallel with each other, and sometimes in opposition to each other. At its best, this approach delivered a good range of relevant services to people in the community; at its worst, it led to examples of poor communication; no communication; no collaboration, and a catalogue of human disasters where people in desperate need 'fell between various stools', sometimes with tragic consequences. Report after report stressed the importance of multi-agency working and professional collaboration. This manual is therefore to be located within this multi-professional context and seeks to be 'at home' on the reading list of any student seeking to enter a 'people work' profession or career.

This is not to say that it will cover all the complexities with which individual professions need to grapple in their training. There will still be the need for more detailed study of subject-specific texts. This manual will provide, however, a basic grounding and introduction to key themes that are common to all people work and will serve as a springboard to further study.

TIP! As you go through the manual, think carefully about how the issues being raised apply to you, your work and your life.

What do values do?

We have emphasized the importance of values, but to understand more fully *why* they are so important, it can be helpful to examine what values actually do, what different roles they play at different times and in different ways. What follows is a quick look at these issues and is far from complete or comprehensive.

Values motivate

So much of what we do in life is driven by our values. For example, talented members of the caring professions who could earn much more in the commercial world are likely to have chosen their career direction on the basis of such values as compassion and dignity. Had they not subscribed to such values, their career choice may well have been very different.

In addition, we can see that people's political views and allegiances will be shaped in large part by values. This applies at the broad political level in terms of party politics, but also in relation to 'micropolitics' – that is, the subtle power dynamics that operate at the level of interpersonal dynamics in the workplace, in family life and in the community. Indeed, conflicts that arise in these contexts will often be rooted in a clash of values. When discussing conflict, people often refer to the concept of a 'personality clash' but, in reality, it is generally more about a clash of values than actual personality (although a person's values will often be part of what we regard as their personality – for example, a person we describe as kind is no doubt someone who subscribes to the value of kindness or compassion).

This can even reach extreme levels – for example when, for political or other causes, some people are prepared to kill, risk their own lives or even take their own lives. That is how powerful a motivator values can be.

Values sustain

Why is it that, when people are under immense pressure, possibly even close to breaking point, they somehow manage to find the strength to keep going? What is it that keeps them committed to seeing things through? The answer, of course, is values. It is the beliefs and principles that they hold dear that sustain us and stop us from giving in, such is the sustenance that values can offer.

It is for this reason that people working under high levels of pressure and in a culture of low morale are wise not to lose sight of their values – indeed, it is at such times that their values are likely to be of most benefit. Unfortunately, though, in such circumstances, low morale can breed negativity, defeatism and cynicism and, in doing so, create distance between us and our values (Thompson, 2025). At that point, the danger is that a vicious circle can arise: the more defeatist we become, the more likely we are to lose sight of our values, and the more we lose sight of our values, the less well equipped we are to tackle the problems that are making us feel so negative in the first place.

Values keep us honest

Criminal and unethical behaviours are, of course, not uncommon across societies. A common question in this regard is: Why do some people behave in such socially unacceptable ways? Sociologist Emile Durkheim turned this on its head and asked: Why do the vast majority of people *not* behave in that way? (Durkheim, 1938). So, rather than focusing on what makes certain people engage in anti-social behaviour, he wanted to examine what stops most of us from doing so? And, of course, the short answer was the set of values that we are socialized into as part of our upbringing. Our values keep us honest.

It is no coincidence that professions generally have codes of ethics. The power base of professions can do harm as well as good, and so the statements of values that feature in codes of ethics are ways of trying to ensure professional integrity – in other words, to keep professional practice honest as far as possible.

Values bring people together

A wide range of groups, clubs, societies, associations and organizations exist because people who share the same values have come together precisely because of those shared values. This includes political parties, campaign groups, trade unions, charities and voluntary organizations, as well as many other such collections of people with common aims. The common aims come from, and are sustained by, common values.

The solidarity that such groupings tend to engender can be of great benefit in terms of mutual support, achieving goals and making a positive difference. Consider how impoverished the workplace would be if trade unions had never existed, workers' rights had never emerged and so many of the workplace protections we now enjoy had never been established.

Values set people apart

Unfortunately, values can be a source of not only solidarity, but also of division, conflict and strife. Consider, for example, how differing religious values (or differing interpretations of religious values) have – both currently and historic-ally – been the basis of bloody and murderous conflicts. People on either side may have believed that they were 'fighting the good fight' in line with their principles and beliefs, but it is clear that the consequences have been anything but good in many cases.

This is not specific to values. It is a characteristic of how groups work that bringing some people together in unison also has the effect of setting them apart from others, with the potential for conflict. This brings into sharp focus the value of diversity, of seeing difference and variety as a social asset and not automatically as the basis for hostility, mistrust and rejection. However, it highlights the importance of developing a good understanding of values and how they affect everybody's lives in a variety of ways.

Values define us

Or, to be more accurate, they are *part* of our identity. What makes us who we are involves a number of dimensions, but values is clearly one of them. Our values in part shape our identity and how we fit into the world. They can therefore be regarded as aspects of spirituality. They are part of how we find meaning in the world and how we develop a sense of purpose and direction and who and what we feel connected to. They shape our worldview.

At certain times, our spirituality can be challenged, our values put to the test. An example of this is what is known as 'moral distress'. It refers to situations where we may be called upon to take steps that run counter to our values (as part of our job, for example). The result can be very strong feelings of discomfort that, in certain circumstances, can leave us questioning our values and, as part of that, questioning who we are.

It should be clear, then, that values are certainly not just the wishy-washy abstract concepts that so many people regard them as – they are vitally important influences on our thoughts, feelings and actions.

Introducing the values debate

If you are already familiar with the existing literature, you will recognize that various authors have struggled with how most effectively to explore values issues and their importance for practice. Shardlow (1998), for example, famously likened the enterprise to that of trying to catch a slippery fish: no sooner do you think you have grasped it than it wriggles free and you are left with oily scales on your hands and an embarrassed look on your face. A few years later, Woodbridge and Fulford (2004) talked about the 'squeaky wheel' principle which suggests that we notice values only when they cause problems – for example, when they are in conflict.

Another popular image likens our awareness of values to our breathing. To breathe is an automatic, autonomic feature of our lives without which we would not survive, and because we do not need consciously to decide whether we breathe or not, we take it for granted. So too with the values that shape our lives and our behaviour: they are simply and essentially *us*. We do not need to take them out to examine them every day; they are part of the 'very fibre of our being' that shapes who we are and how we behave.

There is a further aspect to this we will explore later, namely the wider context of the values debate. Important though our individual values are, we need also to understand that there are wider professional, societal and political values that shape our work and our understanding of society that are of fundamental importance to all people work. Our discussion of anti-discriminatory practice will explore these issues in more detail.

In the meantime, let us return to the vivid images we have just introduced. Each of these images has something important to say to us but, for those who are hoping to go into people work, the story cannot end there. One of the core requirements within any people work training should be that of 'reflective practice' (Schön, 1983, 1987; Thompson and Thompson, 2023). This basic tenet insists that we become aware of who we are and the impact we have upon others precisely because of the way in which our values have such a strong influence upon us and affect the ways in which we engage with others. We need to be aware of our values because there is a distinct chance that, if we are not, we might do more harm than good to the very people who come to us for help and advice. In short, we might become part of the problem and not part of a solution.

There will be times when we grapple with values issues, and it will feel like trying to catch the slippery fish because these issues are not always easy or straightforward. There will be times when our attention is caught by the 'squeaking wheel' and we are pulled up with a jolt as our values-based assumptions are challenged. And we will need on a regular basis to emulate the singer, dancer or musician whose capacity to be aware of, *and control*, their breathing is essential to their professional performance.

One further point needs to be made before we explore these issues in more detail. Each reader of this manual will be bringing with them a wide variety of individual factors that will have an impact upon how you respond to the issues being raised. These factors include your:

- age, gender, class, sexual orientation and ethnicity or 'race';
- strengths and limitations and how these have affected your life (this is sometimes referred to as being 'disabled' or 'non-disabled', but these can be unhelpful concepts if used inappropriately);
- political views or affiliations;
- experience of being in a particular community or stratum of society, especially if this has contributed to your being disadvantaged or discriminated against in any way;
- experience of giving help and receiving help, especially in a professional context; and, finally
- your particular chosen worldview that provides meaning and purpose for your life, and which, for some, may include a religious faith. It will be argued later that this meaning-making aspect of our lives is often overlooked in practice,

something that the current debate about spirituality (in its widest sense) is seeking to address.

All of these factors will combine into a particular 'lens' or 'prism' through which you will interpret what you read on these pages. In other words, everything that has contributed to your own value base will of necessity be involved in your grappling with the issues being raised in this manual, and the impact they have upon you. Some of these aspects will have been absorbed by you without you realizing, and their impact upon you will perhaps have not been examined. Other aspects may be the result of conscious choice and may have had a profound impact upon your whole value base (for example, giving your allegiance to a political party, interest group or to a faith community).

There is also, however, a mirror image to be considered. The same set of factors that combine to impact upon your interpretation of, and engagement with, the issues raised in this manual will also have had an impact upon us as its authors. Tempting though it may be to assume that, once these words appear on the printed page, they automatically have a distinctive, self-evident higher-level validity and 'truth', the reality is different. Like every other writer, we as authors are looking through the prism of our experience and through the lens of the factors that contribute to our humanity. It is therefore important that you, as the reader, are aware of at least some of these factors, the limitations they impose and the influence they have had upon your thinking.

Consider this statement from one of the present authors (Bernard):

I am a white, heterosexual, male who has entered the 'silver-power' era of life (much preferred to grey power!). I have had a varied career in 'people work' which has included leadership of faith communities; probation work; marriage guidance counselling and family mediation, and most recently social work education. I have a strong working-class background that espoused the values of hard work, avoiding going into debt, and being able to do something 'useful' with one's life. From somewhere I imbibed the conviction that humanity would be at its best when differences and variety are celebrated and not denied, and I remember recoiling in horror when very young (without being able to articulate why) whenever I heard racist or homophobic sentiments being expressed. My links with faith communities have given me a sense of awe and mystery and the powerful nature of music in all its wonderful forms. Faith community involvement also quickened my sense of social justice, and a sense of guilt that I was materially better off than so many others, a feeling that still lingers whenever I buy a new car. My original impulse to become a leader of a faith community had its origin in a talk given by a woman of miniscule stature, but enormous convictions who described how she worked among the poor and destitute with little thought of her own needs or aspirations: it was enough to be of service to those in desperate need. Similarly impressive was the Roman Catholic nun who talked about living 'amidst the troubles' of Northern Ireland, and whose response to seeing thousands of nails littered across a main road, intended to cause maximum disruption to the mainly protestant community, was stated simply in the few telling words: 'It took me two hours to pick them all up'. The potential harm caused by the abuse of power began to dawn on me when I was seven or eight and I realized that the old music teacher I went to for piano lessons was quivering with excitement, not from the passion of my incompetent music making, but from the early stages of grooming. I got out, but how many more didn't or couldn't? And I found much, much later in life that an all-consuming passion could sweep me off my feet and change the direction of my life, at the very moment when I seemed to have achieved social respectability. I remember too the sense of awe and mystery gazing at the first dead body I saw and feeling the anguish of those who had watched helplessly the last hours of a most special person in their lives. I realized that questions of meaning and purpose in life had to be faced and not shunned if I was to gain any sense of wholeness. And I remember the times when, as a man, I have cried – sometimes in front of others – realizing slowly that that was not something to be ashamed of, and that there are other, more authentic, patterns of masculinity than the macho bravura that often surrounded me.

The statement you have just read more or less wrote itself. It was not carefully crafted or planned – the words tumbled onto the screen, and no attempt has been made to polish or re-order them to give them academic respectability. All being well, they have given you a brief pen portrait and some hints about what made him 'tick'. Importantly, this pen picture will give you an insight into some of the values that made him what he was.

Reflective moment

Consider for a moment what your 'personal statement' might look like. We will return to this idea later.

The point being made here is to give an example of the very human and personal dimension of values and the way they affect how we live and treat others. In some ways, our experiences can open up, deepen and enrich our value base. In Bernard's case, it sharpened his sense of social justice, the celebration of diversity and the ways in which risk taking and meaning making were central to his life. By contrast, other experiences may have closed down and impoverished his capacity to relate to other people: those who do not work hard or who seem to choose a lifestyle of debt or abuse their power and responsibility. The point for anyone engaged in people work, the present authors included, is that, unless some of these issues are honestly acknowledged and tackled, they are likely to get in the way of the duty of care and the values of respect and dignity we owe to all those that we come into professional contact with.

For some people, of course, some of their attitudes are so entrenched, and they are so unwilling to tackle their demons, that they will never be suited to people work in any shape or form. That is precisely why many professions like policing, nursing, probation and social work, for example, have such stringent selection procedures. But, for all of us who engage in this type of work, and who have been deemed 'safe and ready to practise', the responsibility still remains to become reflective and self-aware so that we can deliver the high-quality service to others to which they are rightly entitled, without getting burdened with the worker's 'baggage'.

We have adopted this approach because we would like to engage with you at a variety of levels as you reflect on the issues raised in this manual and other texts that tackle the issue of values. There needs to be an intellectual understanding of values, and a strong knowledge base to underpin professional practice. This manual seeks to help you develop a clear understanding, and to provide a challenging and thought-provoking commentary on this important topic. It also seeks to provide a context in which you can reflect upon the professional value base of the work you undertake or the career you seek to pursue. Whatever our personal 'take' may be on countless issues, when we enter a particular profession or career we will be expected to embrace and work within a professional value base and framework that sets out clearly what those who use the service can be entitled to expect.

Then again, the work we do has to be seen within the societal and community context in which people live and work and conduct their lives. There are some values issues that at times seem like clashing tectonic plates in society, where some of the great 'isms' (racism; sexism; classism; ageism; heterosexism; disablism, for example) still have their champions and need to be challenged. In the context of all of this, however daunting it may feel at times, stands the uniqueness of each one of us, the personal and individual 'take' on things, and the individual prism or lens through which we not only view the world, but also base our actions and behaviour. This resonates within us at an emotional level as well as the intellectual level. We are what we feel, just as much as what we think or what we do, and because in all people work the most important thing we bring to our work is ourselves, it is important that we do justice to what it means to be fully human. A key part of that is self-awareness, and so it is to that we now turn.

Self-awareness

Of course, we don't know who you are; we know nothing at all about you. The only thing we can assume is that, by picking up this manual, you have something of an interest, a fascination even, for this complex but exciting topic.

One of the authors (Bernard) vividly remembers two comments made by students early on in their degree studies:

> 'I thought my values were "spot on" until I began to study the subject more closely, and now I'm not so sure.'

> 'I just can't seem to get my head round all this values stuff; why does everyone keep banging on about it all the time?'

When he talked to each of them a year later, they both agreed on one thing: that the debate about values and its implication for their practice was the most important aspect of the whole course as far as they were concerned.

That is a bold claim, but many educators would have been delighted to hear it stated. Values are that important, and a consideration of them is rightly central to professional training and education in so many disciplines. We hope to show you throughout this manual that values are at the very heart of the helping enterprise, whether in the caring professions or in a management and leadership context – indeed, anywhere that an advanced level of people skills is required.

Many of us are familiar with being visitors or tourists in a strange city. We open up our newly acquired tourist map with equal measures of excitement and foreboding. We realize that we cannot even begin to work out how to get to some of the places on our list of top ten attractions until we work out on the map where we are now. Until that important discovery has been made, any attempt at further progress is out of the question.

We need to engage in a very similar activity when we begin to talk about values in professional practice. Although there is a body of knowledge that we need to acquire in order to become effective in our chosen field – we need a clear understanding of the legal underpinnings, for example, and to know what we must or must not do in certain situations – but ultimately the most important tool of the trade is ourselves. Who we are, and everything that makes us the complex personalities we have become, these are intimately caught up with our practice.

Key point

Until we are aware of our pride and our prejudice, our successes and our failures, our hopes and our fears (to name but a few on the list), we will not realize that who we really are can impact upon the people we seek to support and may perhaps even help.

In other words, until you understand what you mean by 'values' and how these values fundamentally affect the work you do or hope to do, you cannot even begin to engage safely in the tasks involved in being a competent professional.

Just think for a moment about some of the examples we have mentioned:

■ *Our pride*: People may be very proud of themselves and their achievements in life and be particularly proud of their children. But, if they assume that all people are, or should be, proud of themselves, they may come across to someone who has very low self-esteem, or who hates the way their children have turned out, as being judgemental and disapproving.

■ *Our prejudice*: It is a fundamental insight into the human condition that we all have prejudices to some degree, and that these can deeply affect our behaviour towards others. Unless we have as clear a picture as possible about our own prejudices, we will not be able to stop them getting in the way of our delivering a high-quality service.

■ *Our successes*: The concept, let alone the experience, of being successful, is by no means familiar territory to everyone. Many people who come through the doors of an organization where they are seeking help with personal or family problems are likely to feel anything but successful. It is all too easy to let our own sense of success become apparent so powerfully that it makes those who come to us for help feel worse about themselves.

■ *Our failures*: Most, if not all, of us will have experienced failure of some sort in our personal or professional lives. Those of us who have been divorced, for example, may not have come to terms fully with the sense of failure that often accompanies this experience. We may have some guilt feelings sloshing around inside us deep down, and we may find these rising to the surface when talking with people going through similar experiences. It is sometimes very tempting to give advice based on our (limited, but painful) experience, or to avoid really listening to the other person because it is too painful for us to deal with.

■ *Our hopes and our fears*: We all have them, of course. Are you able to give some examples from your own experience to illustrate these? If you can, it would be helpful to note them down.

From these few and very obvious examples, we have begun to explore some of the values that go to make up ourselves as individuals. Some people, for example, would express the following value statements about their own lives:

■ It is important to be successful in life;
■ Partners should stay together for the sake of their children.

Clearly, they would need to be aware how these values could impact upon the people who come to them for help, so that they do not impose their own values upon them.

> **Reflective moment**
>
> Try making a list, based on what we have discussed so far, of your own values. Jot down a few statements about yourself that you feel express the values you hold.

Being aware of our values and their potential and actual impact is therefore an important part of self-awareness. This was captured in Ancient Greece when travellers who made their way to the Oracle at Delphi for some wise insight into the future were confronted at the entrance with the injunction: know yourself.

What this means is that it is important that we are aware of ourselves, our attitudes and values, and the ways in which they can affect other people. A key part of this is the process known as 'locating yourself'. Locating ourselves, however, has wider connotations than the issues we have so far discussed. How we experience life can depend upon a wide range of factors, such as gender, race, class, sexuality, disability and many more. These are important issues we need to explore.

TIP! Values operate in a social context so, when considering values, we need to think sociologically – that is, be prepared to tune in to the wider social picture and not limit ourselves to individual factors.

Before we invite you to explore this notion of 'locating yourself', it will be helpful for us, as authors, to be prepared to do likewise. Bernard's comments above give you quite a clear picture of 'where he is coming from' and the next paragraph should do the same for Neil.

I am a white, non-disabled male from a working-class background. My father died when I was three, and so I was one of four brothers being brought up in a family where a meagre widow's pension was the main income. Until I left home to go to university, we lived in a deprived area with a high crime rate and extensive social problems. In the absence of a father figure, my uncle was a major influence on me. He combined compassion with a commitment to social justice (reflecting his trade union background). I am heterosexual and I have a grown-up daughter who has a visual impairment. I married at an early age and have not once regretted that. My interest in, and passion for, languages led me in the direction of wanting to be a speech therapist, but this evolved into being a social worker, and my interest in languages evolved into an interest in communication that remains a major focus of my work to this day. I reached the level of professor in the academic world but decided that I could make more of a positive impact on practice in a freelance capacity. At the time of writing, I have just passed the 28th anniversary of commencing in that role, and that too is something I have never regretted. My passion is for making a positive difference through problem solving, empowerment and promoting learning.

Obviously, we cannot predict how you will have responded to the limited amount of information we have given you, but there is a fair chance that how you will have reacted will depend on how you feel Neil may be able to identify with you. So, among your many reactions, there could be the following:

- How can a man understand where I am coming from as a woman?
- As a disabled person, I don't think he'll have any idea about my situation.
- How do I know, as a gay/lesbian person, that he won't be full of homophobic attitudes like so many other heterosexual people?
- I feel very comfortable knowing this, because he's just like me.
- He seems to have spent a fair bit of his life in 'ivory towers', so what can he tell me about real life?
- He belongs to the dominant white culture. So, as a black person, I shall be expecting to find evidence of racist attitudes in this manual.

These are but a few of the reactions that Neil's statement could possibly have provoked in you (and, likewise, Bernard's statement earlier). In our discussions about values, it is important to recognize at the outset that the assumptions and value judgements we make about each other are very real and very powerful. Part of the value base we shall be exploring below is about valuing diversity. This means that all of us involved with this manual, authors and readers alike, need to acknowledge where each of us is coming from and see what impact this might have on the issues we are discussing.

To take this a bit further, from our own 'self-locations' given above, we need to be aware that people who are different from us in all sorts of ways will have differing perspectives and differing experiences that are valid, and which we need to respect. We also need to take on board the fact that we represent, simply by being white, non-disabled, heterosexual males, a wide range of oppressive behaviours in society against women, disabled people and those with a different sexual orientation. And not only do we represent such behaviours; there is a possibility that, unless we are scrupulously careful, we will display some of these attitudes and behaviours that others find so oppressive – we will allow the discriminatory ideas that were part of the context in which we were brought up to undermine our practice.

That is why values are so important: we all risk offering to people a poor-quality, possibly even a dangerous, service if we are not fully aware of how our values can affect how we behave towards other people.

The process of locating ourselves has other dimensions too. Our value base as individuals is profoundly affected by the views and opinions we hold. There is a wide range of issues that we can use as a kind of litmus test that helps us to uncover what are the values that are important to us.

Reflective moment

Are there (or do you anticipate there being) any aspects of your work where your personal values may come into particular conflict with those of a person you are supporting? Are there any aspects of practice you feel you could not or should not undertake because of the clash with your own values?

Conclusion

This first chapter of the manual has focused upon you and the values you hold. People professionals come in all shapes and sizes and from many different cultures and backgrounds. Some belong to political parties; some belong to faith communities; some are disabled; some are LGBTQ+. Individually, we probably hold as diverse a range of opinions and attitudes as the rest of the population, even though we are united by a common desire to undertake the complex, yet rewarding, tasks of making a positive difference to people who are struggling with one or more aspects of their lives or who rely on us for guidance and leadership.

If you have stayed with us so far in this chapter, you will have begun to gain a clearer picture of who you are and what matters to you. Importantly, you will have gained insights into where the 'shoe might rub' in your practice – that is, where your own personal values might come into conflict with one or more aspects of your work situation.

As we said at the outset, all of this is important work to help you locate yourself on the map, in order to understand 'where you are at' in terms of the values you hold. As your career unfolds, you may find some of your personal values changing of course, and perhaps that is only to be expected. For the moment, however, you have looked into the mirror and begun to see yourself for who you really are. The next step is to ask the much wider question about what set of values underpin professional practice. This will be the focus of Chapter 2.

Key point

If I am not clear about my own values, then I am likely to become part of the problem and not part of the solution.

Exercise 1

Consider the list of statements that you are invited to either agree or disagree with. After deciding, think carefully about what this says about your values and how they make you who you are, your self-location as we have called it.

Making sense of values

Introduction

In the previous chapter we concentrated on your personal mirror, encouraging you to spend a lot of time reflecting on what your own personal value system looks and feels like. In this chapter, we begin to paint on a broader canvas and raise some important issues about the people professions. Is there a set of values to which all people workers need to subscribe in order to undertake their responsibilities professionally and effectively?

The answer to this question is a resounding 'yes', but as you have probably guessed by now, it is not particularly straightforward to get to grips with the issues. We mentioned briefly Shardlow's comment about values being 'slippery'. He expressed it in these terms:

> Getting to grips with … values and ethics is rather like picking up a live, large and very wet fish out of a running stream. Even if you are lucky enough to grab a fish, the chances are that just when you think you have caught it, the fish will vigorously slither out of your hands and jump back in the stream.
>
> (Shardlow, 1998, p. 23)

Shardlow is reminding us that many of us find it much easier to get on with the task in hand and to do something, rather than stand back and ask disconcerting questions such as:

DOI: 10.4324/9781003689614-3

- Why am I doing this?
- How do my own values affect what I am doing?
- Should I be doing this?
- What does the person I am working with think, feel, want, need?

He is also pointing out that the values debate itself is quite complex, with some of it at times seeming obscure and imprecise. What could and should be an exciting and fundamental topic can become sidelined if people do not make the effort to explore some of the complexities.

The values debate

It is worth spending time briefly tracing some of the main themes in the debate about values. We acknowledge at the outset that this will inevitably seem sketchy and incomplete. It is. All we are seeking to do here is to highlight some of the themes and to point you in the direction of key material that explores these issues in greater depth.

Much of what we have covered so far may be said to focus upon the individual worker and the values that underpin and inform professional practice. While this is crucially important, it is not the whole story, not by any means.

More recent writers, and indeed much of current professional education and training. Place these individual values in the context of what is happening within society generally. More and more professionals are now being encouraged to consider the impact of society upon the people who traditionally are the ones who need help and support from human services professionals. Consider the following examples:

- A black person complains that, in spite of dozens of job applications, no work can be found;
- A woman looking after three small children single handedly complains that she simply has not got enough money;
- A disabled person describes the 101 different ways in which access to services, transport and facilities is denied;
- A gay man complains that he is constantly being victimized;
- A woman who has experienced domestic violence complains bitterly that it is still a man's world.

Think for a moment about each of these statements – what do you feel an appropriate response might be from anyone hearing these comments? You might find it helpful to jot down the main points you think are significant.

As you reflect on these issues, you will quickly realize that underlying the complaints made by each of the people in the examples above is an aspect of society that is fundamentally unfair and unjust. It is not just that individual black people experience racist attitudes, or that individual women experience sexist behaviour, or that individual disabled people are discriminated against, or that LGBTQ+ people experience individual harassment. That is bad enough. It is more serious than that. We are now realizing more and more that society itself is structured, or skewed, in a particular way that works to the advantage of some and the disadvantage of others (Thompson, 2018a).

A range of professionals frequently work with people who are disadvantaged in all sorts of ways and are experiencing problems and difficulties that are not really their fault. If the professionals concerned do not realize this, they could easily make matters worse – for example, by blaming a family for the poverty they are experiencing, when in fact they are victims of the way society is structured. The temptation to 'pathologize' people with problems – in other words, to assume that it is all their fault and due to some defect within them or their personality or their upbringing – must be resisted if we are to become part of the answer, instead of part of the problem.

We have begun to identify some key issues that have a major place in the contemporary debate about values. These may be labelled as:

- racism;
- sexism;
- ageism;
- disablism;
- classism; and
- heterosexism;

and the overarching concepts are discrimination and oppression. These are not the only forms of discrimination and nor do they operate in isolation. They will often interact or intersect in complex ways – what is often referred to as 'intersectionality' (May, 2015).

Societies are structured in such a way that certain groups of people are disadvantaged and oppressed, and this has a major impact upon them as individuals, as families and as communities. Life chances are diminished; life expectancy may be reduced; resilience may be undermined; and a capacity to be creative or to cope with problems and difficulties may be reduced.

We can now begin to understand why contemporary practice has, at its core, the crucial values of anti-discriminatory practice, although they are not without controversy. They are important because they make serious demands upon workers to understand the complex and at times oppressive aspects of the society in which their practice takes place, and to make sure that they produce carefully formulated strategies that not only take account of these oppressive aspects but also make a serious attempt to counteract them.

The growing literature on this topic has highlighted the importance of understanding the complexity of these issues. It helps if we can think of them in three separate but constantly interacting dimensions – that is:

- *The personal level* – issues relating to the individual, their views and attitudes, including prejudices;
- *The cultural level* – the shared meanings, unwritten rules and taken-for-granted assumptions that cultures are based on; and
- *The structural level* – characterized by how society is structured in terms of social divisions, such as class, gender, race/ethnicity and so on.

This is the basis of Thompson's PCS analysis (Thompson, 2018a, 2018b; Thompson and Cox, 2025), and all people workers will find that their practice will be developed significantly by exploring the implications of this important analytical tool. This is because it:

i. Highlights the complex and dynamic nature of discrimination and the oppression it gives rise to (the personal is influenced by the cultural which, in turn, is influenced by the structural).
ii. Warns us against taking too narrow a view and limiting our understanding of discrimination to matters of personal prejudice (the personal level) by casting light on how cultural and structural factors also have a key role to play.
iii. Alerts us to the role of wider cultural factors (such as stereotypes, discriminatory assumptions and forms of language) in which the personal level is located or 'embedded'.
iv. Shows how the cultural level itself is embedded within the structural level, the way in which society is not a level playing field due to the divisions that make up its structure.

The value of PCS analysis is that it gives us a framework or analytical tool to make sense of the complex interactions that lead to discrimination and oppression. It helps us to tune in to the wider social context and, in so doing makes us better

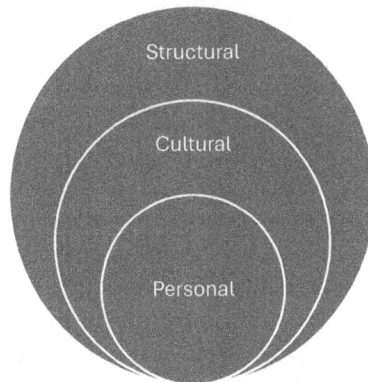

Figure 2.1 PCS analysis

equipped to understand, and challenge, racism, sexism, ageism and the other forms of discrimination that have oppressive consequences for the people affected by them.

Key point

The crucial role of the worker lies in promoting equality and social justice, rather than reinforcing or exacerbating the inequalities that already exist in society and in people's lives. Traditional approaches have tended to pay little or no attention to issues of inequality, discrimination or oppression and can leave people feeling alienated, devalued and disempowered.

An overview of the values debate

The issue of how we should treat each other as human beings has exercised people's thinking and behaving probably from time immemorial. From a western Eurocentric perspective, there are important strands to this discussion that deserve mention. The Judaeo-Christian tradition has had an enormous influence. Within the understanding of the three main monotheistic faiths, human beings owe their existence to the Divine Being (Allah; God; 'Adonay' in Muslim, Christian and Jewish traditions, respectively), who gives to each and every person a uniqueness and specialness that reflects the goodness of the Creator. A phrase often used to capture this view is 'the image of God'. It then follows that, if human beings are made in the image of God, then it is incumbent upon everyone to treat everyone else with that dignity and respect that reflects their ultimate origin.

Human history of course is littered with examples that show that exactly the opposite has often been the case. Religious wars have been as fierce and vitriolic as can be imagined, conducted in the very name of the One who is believed to have created them. But the basic principle has remained: each person is seen as a child of God and is infinitely precious precisely because of that and must be treated accordingly.

The Judaeo-Christian tradition has also developed a strong sense of social justice, recognizing that, for society to reflect its Creator, some fundamental changes have to be made. Therefore, in the Jewish prophetic writings that are now 'jointly owned' by Christian tradition, there are strong claims to justice, with urgent demands 'for swords to be beaten into ploughshares' (Micah 4, 1–5), and for 'justice to flow like a never-ending stream' (Amos 5, 21–24). Many of these prophetic strands were taken up by the founder of Christianity and have become in many ways part of the fabric of western cultural and religious heritage. These include not only the command to love our neighbours as ourselves (Luke 10, 27), but also some of the most vivid stories and parables that Jesus gave to illustrate the point. The Good Samaritan (Luke 10, 30f), the parable of the sheep and the goats (Matthew 25, 31f) and the parable of the wedding feast (Luke 14, 15–24) all reflect the same value base and the same moral imperative: every person is important and precious in the eyes of God, and this must be reflected in the ways in which we treat each other as sisters and brothers. Or, to continue the theme of the wedding feast, no one should be excluded from the banquet or be deemed unworthy to attend, unless of course they deliberately choose not to join in that particular party.

In our multicultural society, there has been a strengthening of these tenets from the perspective of other faith traditions. Islam, for example, stemming from Judaeo-Christian roots, places strong emphasis upon the merciful nature of Allah, and the demands upon those who live in obedience to the rule of Allah to demonstrate mercy, kindness and compassion to others (Chapter 2, vv 110; 148; 177; 215). One of the five pillars of Islam, for example, encourages 'zakat', the giving of alms to the poor. Other faith perspectives are no less demanding. Buddhism and Hinduism make similar demands for peaceful relationships between people. Leaving aside for one moment the singular failure of many religious systems to put their beliefs fully into practice, it is nevertheless important to note carefully the contributions they make to the value base that underpins (or at least significantly contributes to) contemporary practice.

Alongside these perspectives, other non-religious approaches have an important contribution to make. Although it is not always easy historically to separate the religious and secular strands in the skein of understanding, those for whom religious perspectives do not hold an attraction also have their philosophical champions. Immanuel Kant (1724–1804), for example, is well known for his assertion: 'So act as to treat humanity, whether in your own person or in that of any other, never solely as a means, but always also as an end'. This clearly resonates with the religiously based comment that we should 'love our neighbours as ourselves': everyone has equal value and is entitled to be treated respectfully and with dignity.

Another strand has its origins with two other philosophical giants, David Hume (1711–76) and John Stuart Mill (1806–73) who argued the utilitarian position that says that the benchmark for the morality of any action is the extent to which it achieves more good than harm and brings benefits to the majority. This has clear links into the debate about social justice that is an important strand in much contemporary training for human service workers.

The point being made here is that, whether you look at these issues from a religious or secular perspective, the key themes about valuing and respecting the individual, and seeking to devise social systems that benefit the majority and pay particular attention to the needs of oppressed and downtrodden people, are common melodies that are played with equal conviction in this great symphony of values. Religious and non-religious themes blend and interweave to enhance the fundamental message of the value of each and every human being. They form the foundation of the value base of the helping professions that are the focus of this manual.

> **Reflective moment**
>
> Where do you fit in this picture, religious, secular or perhaps elements of both? Knowing where our values come from can help us understand them more fully.

In the twentieth century there were other influential figures whose contribution to the values debate may be regarded as seminal. There were also important developments in theoretical perspectives that have transformed the values debate for the human services.

The issue of how we should treat other people within a professional helping relationship was explored by a number of workers whose principal interest was in counselling. Carl Rogers (1961), for example, spoke of the importance of 'unconditional positive regard', a phrase that has entered the language of most, if not all, the helping professions. Put at its simplest, it means that we work with people with no strings attached – we offer them 100 per cent attention and take them with the utmost seriousness. We do nothing to undermine their intrinsic value as people, whatever we may feel about their behaviour.

Rogers's emphasis upon the importance of 'empathy' (what it feels like to walk in someone else's shoes) and 'congruence' (being completely genuine and in tune with the other person) are also part of professional parlance and indicate the importance of his contribution to our understanding of key underpinning values that are shared by many, probably all, contemporary helping professions.

TIP! Empathy is an important concept, but many people confuse it with sympathy. Sympathy means sharing another person's feelings. Whereas empathy means recognizing someone's feelings without necessarily sharing them.

Another seminal figure whose name still is regularly cited in the literature is Biestek (1961). He too focused a lot of attention on how individuals should be treated by their professional helpers. (NB: We are using the word 'treated' here with some degree of caution. In this context it is intended to have a neutral feel to it, although in the 1960s there was a dominant medical model that assumed that people could be effectively 'treated' by such interventions.) His seven principles again find their way into the literature and continue to resonate with workers today. The principles he articulated were:

- individualization;
- purposeful expression of feelings;
- controlled emotional involvement;
- acceptance;
- confidentiality;
- non-judgemental attitude; and
- client self-determination.

Again, it is easy to see how these principles reflect the value base that has already been articulated in this chapter. They represent both an ideal towards which all workers and helpers should aim in their professional practice, and the benchmark against which their practice will always be measured (for a succinct summary and discussion of these seven principles, see Thompson, 2024a, Chapter 5). It is worth noting in passing that Biestek himself had a strong religious background and faith. This is another example of how some of the core underpinning values that are now espoused by a much wider audience have their origins in a religious context.

Important though these person-centred approaches have been, and still are, to all people work, some wider perspectives were brought into the debate at a later stage that have proved hugely influential and important. To these developments we must now turn.

Taking a wider view

Biestek and Rogers laid the foundation stones for one-to-one practice, and recent developments have widened rather than replaced them. Thompson (2024a) makes an observation that is relevant to all people work when he reminds us about the 'person-centred' nature of all human services activities, where there is a focus on supporting the unique individual in dealing with personal and social challenges that arise in the course of their lives.

This is important to note, especially in the light of the critique that emerged in the latter half of the last century. This critique pointed out that there was a wider context in which people's 'problems' could be located, and that if attention was focused purely and simply on the individuality and specificity of the person's 'problem' there was a serious risk of missing vitally important dimensions to the concerns and issues that people were presenting. The social and political context, therefore, became increasingly important factors in the 'human equation', and counterbalanced the tendency within an individualistic approach to pathologize people who came for help. In other words, this would be to imply that their 'problems' are all to do with some defect in their personality and/or their approach to life. But once you begin to pathologize people's difficulties, it is but a small step before you enter the 'blame culture'. This is another example of the value of PCS analysis as a tool for appreciating the wider cultural and structural aspects.

A very clear example of this would be work-based stress. It is far too easy to respond to someone who is complaining of stress at work in a way that suggests that this is due to some weakness or deficiency on their part, with a tacit warning that they need to do better in future. It may be the case, however, that the demands of the job are wholly unrealistic, and that the responsible response would be to take clear look at what is being expected of this person and undertake a risk assessment of the role (Thompson, 2024b).

A clear example of this is how we regard people who have massive debt problems. There are unquestionably important areas of individual responsibility and accountability that are at the core of each debtor's difficulties. But if the debate stays at that level and refuses to take into account the cultural expectations of taking out easy loans, where people can be bombarded with opportunities to borrow 'x' thousand pounds from banks and building societies, not to mention unscrupulous loan dealers, then we lose sight of the very real pressures to which people under stress can easily succumb. We live in a society where consumerism is a major factor in people's lives, and where advertisers target young people with a wide range of branded goods, especially at Christmas. To resist such pressures requires at times almost superhuman effort, and it is no wonder that many people find the pathway into debt frighteningly slippery and largely beyond their control.

Youth workers could provide countless other examples. Young people at the critical stage in their development when they are exploring their values, lifestyles and worldviews often find themselves drawn into situations which, from an 'adult' perspective, are fraught with risk. And yet, for many young people, to stand against the encouragement of peer pressure to engage in certain behaviours requires a level of maturity and courage that is often difficult to achieve when, developmentally, peer acceptance and group identity are their dominant psychological needs.

The point could be illustrated from many other perspectives. The sort of culture and group we belong to tends both to reflect, and then significantly to influence our own attitudes and behaviours. Individual choice and responsibility are tempered by the contexts in which we live, and it is cause for no surprise if the cost of standing out against the crowd is a price many find difficult and, at times, impossible to pay.

These are a few examples of some of the ways in which the works of Biestek and Rogers were not so much challenged as if they were wrong but were placed into a wider framework. If Biestek's and Rogers's insights were the core values and principles for one-to-one help and support, the social and political context formed an outer ring, encircling and widening the framework for understanding people's difficulties, and finding ways to respond to them effectively.

There were, however, some more profound perspectives to this critique. It was argued that, if the root of a person's problems lies in wider cultural and structural factors (which, in turn, causes a person to be treated unfairly and to feel downtrodden and disadvantaged), then the solution or response offered to them needs to be at that same level if any changes are to be effected to improve that person's situation. Anything less would be cosmetic, rather than dealing with the root of the problem. It is the ramifications of this powerful insight gave that social work and the other helping professions a wider canvas for understanding, and a deeper theoretical framework for assessing, how most effectively to intervene – or even whether it would be best not to intervene at all (bearing in mind that efforts to help always have the potential to make the situation worse).

This critique of social factors raised deeper issues than the examples so far cited. The challenge was made to the very fabric of society, and how deep strands of fundamental inequality made it impossible for many people to experience the benefits of being regarded as uniquely precious. These strands are now frequently referred to as the great 'isms': sexism; racism; classism; disablism; heterosexism; and so on.

Familiar though these concepts may be to many, the neat labelling of them as 'isms' runs the risk of diminishing their impact. In many ways, these insights took people by storm when they first began to be discussed and debated. They were fiercely controversial, and rightly so, because they provided powerful examples of the very issues that needed to be challenged and addressed.

TIP! Be careful not to make the mistake of equating a commitment to challenging discrimination and oppression to a simplistic 'political correctness' approach that fails to do justice to the complexities involved.

The danger now is that, with much progress undoubtedly having been made in many of these areas, and the language of this debate having entered into the main-stream discussion, we begin to regard them as less important, and less challenging to our own practice. And yet they remain crucially important for contemporary people work: they remind us what can happen when the central value base that is being articulated and described in this manual is not respected and put into pro-fessional practice. Progress is not inevitable, even if legislation sharpens people's awareness of what behaviours are now deemed to be unlawful.

The challenge of the great 'isms' was felt most acutely by those who were seen to be the most powerful in society, principally white, middle/upper class heterosexual men, who assumed their role of power effortlessly, and without an awareness of the shadows that such behaviour cast upon other sections of society. It was inevitable, therefore, that such power bases had to be challenged if there were to be any realignment into a more just and equitable society.

The experience of women is a classic example of this. Women in the UK did not suddenly wake up one morning to find their husbands bringing them a cup of tea and their franchise on the breakfast tray. On the contrary, they had to fight tooth and nail to get their voices heard, and their rights recognized. Power had to be wrested from the dominant male power group in order for a greater equality to be achieved. But this was just the first step of many, and major issues such as the role of women in society and in the family; their control over their own bodies; their right to equal working conditions and equal pay; their opportunities to rise to the very top of the ladder in management and leadership positions: these are issues that are still 'work in progress' in spite of the advances that have been achieved. But, even the phrase 'work in progress' is dangerous, because it understates the very serious struggles and fights that are still needed before women enjoy the equality that is their fundamental and inalienable right as human beings.

Racism is another huge issue where the implications of the value base being described in this manual have still not fully been worked out in our society. It is cer-tainly a salutary experience to look back at the television documentaries relating to the 1950s and to witness the blatant 'colour bar' that blighted the housing and employment opportunities for so many people. Legislation and public opinion have made great strides in the struggle to eradicate such hideous behaviour. But, to pretend that, as a society, we now treat everyone with dignity and respect, regardless of their skin colour or ethnicity, would be to live in a fantasy world. As evidence of this, we have only to consider the developing popularity of far-right organizations and to look at some their campaign literature. Additionally, the whole issue of immigration and asylum seekers, which is a topic of serious debate by some, is also seen by many to be tinged with racist overtones and a refusal to accept that a genuine celebration of diversity can enrich, not diminish, national culture and economic strength. There are also worrying examples of how black people are over-represented in mental health services and prison populations (Blumstein, 2015).

Further dimensions include institutional racism. For example, the Macpherson report (Macpherson, 1999) that came out of the investigation into the murder of Stephen Lawrence in 1993 showed that, in the Metropolitan Police there were not only a range of barriers that prevented black officers from making a steady progress up the promotion ladder. There were also built-in structures and procedures that actively discriminated against minority ethnic members of the Police Service. This report served as a 'wake-up call' for such issues to be addressed. It also has clear implications for all organizations to make sure not only that there are equal opportunities for all sections of a community to apply for posts, but also that attitudes and procedures are not 'skewed' in such a way as to disadvantage people on racial or ethnic grounds. Sadly, there has been no shortage of further examples of institutional racism since that highly significant report, as clearly evidenced by the Black Lives Matter movement.

Classism has probably received less treatment in the literature than other major 'isms'. This may be because it may be seen by some to be of less importance, because it is less well understood or because for many years it was seen by many as the only basis of discrimination. Nevertheless, it deserves careful attention, because it points to the ways in which people can be unduly advantaged or disadvantaged because of their position in the class structures. It has several manifestations, ranging from the upper-class elitism that allows those 'with connections' to move easily into 'higher echelon' educational, employment, business and governmental opportunities (at one end of the spectrum) to the seriously disadvantaged people (at the other end of the spectrum) who experience the 'postcode lottery', who live in economically, educationally and culturally deprived areas and thereby have less opportunity to develop their true potential or have access to a full range of services.

One common phrase that highlights this issue very well is 'postcode lottery'. By this is meant that some people's chances and opportunities to receive high-quality medical care, and also other human services, are often determined by where people live. For example, if you are in a well-paid occupation and can afford to live in a relatively affluent area, you will stand a better chance of receiving high-quality services compared with poor, unemployed people who live in poor conditions in an inner city (Hastings and Matthews, 2011).

Again, as with the other 'isms', classism is important to acknowledge because it highlights ways in which cultural and structural factors can be powerful influences on whether or not people 'get on' and succeed, and whether or not their 'life chances' and 'good health chances' are high or low.

Disablism, by contrast, has gained a higher profile, not least because of the Disability Discrimination Act 1995, which led to far-reaching changes and benefits in everyday life for the population as a whole. Whether the issue is easy access onto public transport or into public buildings; ensuring that educational opportunities are genuinely accessible to everyone, or that employers make sure that their employment policies and procedures are 'disability friendly', the impact has been enormous and has raised awareness of disability issues with the population at large. For many years, activists like Mike Oliver (2009) have been arguing that disabled people tend to be seen first of all as disabled, and then, by way of an afterthought, as people. There has been a history of their being either 'invisible' ('Does she take sugar?') or too visible for comfort (learning-disabled people being refused service in a restaurant; Deaf people not being allowed on aircraft are two examples of this). The change in legislation served as a challenge to many of the stereotypes and prejudices that have held disabled people back from playing their full role in the community and has confronted 'head on' the assumption that to be disabled is to have less to offer than those who are often called by contrast 'able-bodied'.

The difficulty, of course, is when we begin to relax and assume that, because these important developments have taken place, we have reached a position where genuine equality is enjoyed by everyone. People who use a variety of services will be quick to remind us, however, just how far we still need to go before such a claim can be made. Moving in the right direction and arriving at our destination are two different things.

A further change has occurred also in the use of language. For some years now the old terminology of 'spastic', 'handicapped' and 'lunatic' for example has begun to be jettisoned, quite rightly, for labelling and thus being discriminatory. We are now beginning to see, however, that such terms as 'able-bodied' carry similar risks of being value laden and discriminatory against those who, for whatever reason, may not have a fully functional physique. But this is to elevate the physical above other aspects of being human. The truth is that everyone is a complex kaleidoscope of ability and disability; things we are good at and things we can't get the hang of; contributions at which we excel, and things that are simply 'not our scene at all'. This is what lies behind the move to using terms such as disabled/non-disabled as a step in the right direction, but it clearly does not go far enough. Certainly, there would be advantages in talking only about strengths and limitations as far as all of us are concerned, although we must take note that, in some circumstances, the term 'disabled' is an important gate-keeping label to access appropriate additional help, support and benefits. This is also a good example of how we live in a fast-moving world, where attitudes and language are changing in order to reflect the central conviction that society will only fully flourish when everyone is able to work and live to their full potential. There is still a long way to go, however, before this becomes a reality.

Problems associated with heterosexism arise when one section of the population that happens to be by far the numerical majority, not only deems its sexual orientation to be the norm, but then also pillories and labels any different orientations as 'abnormal', 'deviant' and socially unacceptable. The ways in which LGTBQ+ people have been victimized throughout the centuries has been one of the most appalling features of so-called civilized societies. It has also been an issue where some religious organizations and faith communities have fuelled the rhetoric of abuse. Some religious groups have made it clear that, in their view (which they claim is supported by their sacred texts), to deviate from the heterosexual norm, and to share sexual intimacy as an expression of love and commitment with a same-sex partner is evil, reprehensible and damnable.

Clearly, this issue has also been clouded by the ways in which assumptions have been made by some groups about 'abusive tendencies', and the ways in which people may be sexually exploited. Abuse is never acceptable and is anathema as far as the value base of the helping professions is concerned. But the point to stress here is that abuse can and does happen within the heterosexual majority, and that existence of a minority with a different sexual orientation does not mean that all such relationships are by definition abusive.

Ageism is the final example of a great 'ism' that we comment upon briefly in this chapter to 'flesh out' the principles being outlined here. As popularly understood, ageism seems often to be regarded as applying only to the senior generation. This points to ways in which older people are often excluded from various aspects of society simply because of their age. Therefore, older people find it increasingly difficult to find employment if their services have been dispensed with by a previous employer; there are examples of health care rationing, and a general sense that they have become a drain and a burden upon the nation's scant resources. The 'problem' of old age became powerfully articulated in the 1970s when, in America and elsewhere, huge concerns were raised about whether society would be able to afford to support pensioners in any economically viable way.

Fortunately, some countervailing perspectives began to be articulated towards the end of the twentieth century that began to emphasize a more positive and creative understanding of old age, and the contributions that older people can continue to make to the wellbeing of communities in which they live (Sue Thompson, 2025). This of course finds echoes in other cultures where old age is venerated as a source of wisdom and guidance, and where older people are not valued only as economically productive 'units'.

But, the debate about ageism is not to be limited to older age. It can work at the other end of the age scale as well, as Sue Thompson (2005) clearly reminds us. Younger people are often regarded as only half-formed incomplete adults, instead of being human beings and individuals in their own right, and their contributions are consequently disregarded, or patronised. This can happen to young people entering their field of people work, where their youthfulness is interpreted as disqualifying them from being able to make a valuable contribution as professional workers. Ageism therefore needs to be challenged across the whole spectrum, so that the contribution people can make, irrespective of their age, can be welcomed, valued and developed.

This has been a very swift overview of some of the key issues that are important to an understanding of how wider cultural and structural perspectives can, and do, impact upon our understanding of the values debate. To these important issues, there have been three main responses as the values debate has unfolded. The first has been something of a political backlash that became known as 'political correctness' and which has evolved into the modern notion of 'wokeism'. The other two are the equality movement and the development of anti-discriminatory practice as a practice-focused approach to dealing with these complex issues. To all three of these we must now turn.

Political correctness (PC)

The whole genre of political correctness has now become a rich vein of satire and mockery almost on a par with the mother-in-law style humour of previous decades. Comedians and politicians alike regard it as an easy target for a cheap jibe, or for attracting populist sympathies.

There was indeed a period when it could be argued that such a response would be inevitable. The list of things 'you couldn't say' because they were deemed 'not PC' seemed endless, and included:

- Manhole cover;
- Seminal work;
- Black coffee;
- Blackboard; and many more.

What had begun as a serious and challenging 'movement' became pilloried for its inanity; indeed the 'silly examples' that abounded in the popular press almost guaranteed that the underpinning crucial issues would be effortlessly sidelined.

What is at stake here, however, is the power of language, and the ways in which language not only reflects our values but also shapes them. And this takes us right into the heart of the values debate. Some people began to realize that the language to which they had grown accustomed not only reflected some of the oppressive cultural and structural formations in society but also contributed to their continuation. As one means of challenging these problems, therefore – and it was only one of several strategies that were available – the powerful nature of language had to be addressed, and the ways in which certain words were used had to be redefined in order to reflect the value base of celebrating diversity.

In the oppressive context of racism, therefore, it became increasingly important to exercise care when using the word 'black'. As a neutral description of a colour, it is indeed both useful and should not cause offence. There is, after all, only one way of describing the rich variety of colours that Henry Ford offered his new car-buying customers: they had a choice of black, black or black. The notes of caution were sounded because, in many ways, for every time the word 'black' was used as a positive attribute ('My bank statement is in the black – that's excellent news after all the spending I've done lately'), there were many other examples where it was being used with a negative connotation – for example:

- Black mark;
- Black sheep of the family;
- Black Wednesday;
- Black market;
- Black day; and
- Black mood.

In other words, by using the adjective 'black', a strongly negative image was being created, so much so that its racist overtones became unmistakable. Black people were seen as second-class citizens, and the language of 'blackness', in contrast to the assumed purity of 'whiteness', reinforced this prejudice.

This is not to imply that all racist attitudes were caused by such insensitive use of language; it is a much more complex and deep-seated phenomenon. But the use of 'black' to denote inferiority became a major litmus test for a movement that sought to reflect its core values in the everydayness of accurate language. Language use is a key part of how discrimination operates at the cultural level – the C of PCS analysis.

As a commentary on this theme, look up the poem entitled 'White Comedy' by Benjamin Zephaniah that transposes black with white in a powerful way to illustrate how the word black is so often used in a pejorative way.

A similar and parallel issue concerned sexism. Even a cursory glance at linguistic styles and conventions of the early-to-mid twentieth century revealed that it was assumed that the use of 'man' and 'mankind' automatically included women. Indeed, it was so self-evident that even to challenge it seemed risible. And yet a closer scrutiny revealed that the language was far more accurate than had been realized. Society was profoundly sexist in the ways in which the power structures were concerned, and in many ways women were regarded as inferior and second-class citizens, or certainly not distinctive enough to merit any linguistic adjustments. The attempts by some to reflect this by adopting nomenclature such as 'madam chairman' soon were overtaken by a more root and branch approach, that sought to ensure that language was always appropriately inclusive. Therefore, a straightforward set of alternatives grew in popularity, including:

- Chair;
- Humankind;
- Police officer; and
- Firefighter.

We must add to this an increasing sensitivity that not all professional people are necessarily male. Of course, there were cheap jibes made (personhole covers in the road), but the serious issue was how to ensure in the language we use that women's value and status in society are given equal respect in everyday speech, and not just in academic tomes.

Another example of how this process has had an impact may be found within the field of disability where language that was commonplace some 50 or 60 years ago has now been largely expunged from our vocabulary: handicapped, mongol, cretin, for example.

The underlying message in all of this is hugely important for the theme of this manual. If our value base is about valuing people, respecting their individuality, celebrating their diversity and also acknowledging some of the powerful oppressive influences at work at the personal, cultural and structural levels of our society, then the language we use is all important. We can even go so far as to say that our choice of language will either sustain the status quo and maintain the discriminatory impact of society on various groups and members of it or it will begin to effect a change and become a tool of what may be called emancipatory practice. It is as important as that, and those who mock this for being 'merely PC' or 'woke' are playing their part in maintaining the status quo and putting back the time when people's true dignity and worth can be effectively valued and celebrated.

What is needed, then, to develop truly values-based practice, is not a simplistic PC approach that seeks to ban certain words, but, rather, the development of what Thompson (2018c) calls 'linguistic sensitivity' – namely the ability to tune in to when certain forms of language are problematic and use more appropriate, empowering alternatives.

Unfortunately, many people get overanxious about linguistic sensitivity and panic about 'saying the wrong thing'. This is not necessary, as it is simply a process of becoming more and more aware over time which forms of language help and which hinder.

A note on being 'woke'

Interestingly, in recent years, we have seen a parallel development in the way some people have started using the term 'woke'. It was originally introduced as a positive term meaning being alert – or awake – to the injustices associated with discrimination. That is, it referred to having a commitment to social justice, clearly a good thing in terms of the values needed to work effectively and ethically in the people professions, including in a management or leadership position.

However, as so often happens with language (as a vehicle for power), in the right-wing media and elsewhere it has come to be used in a derogatory sense to describe supporters of equality as fanatical, misguided or extremist. When used in this sense, it is clearly an obstacle to social justice and therefore a highly problematic form of language and sadly an example of how misinformation (or deliberate disinformation) can stand in the way of promoting values that are inclusive and have a positive benefit on everyone, especially those in our communities who are disadvantaged and discriminated against.

To a large extent, the situation relating to the use of the word 'woke' is a continuation of the historical development of the concept of political correctness. Whenever we encounter (or use) the term 'woke', we should therefore be very careful to make sure that it is not being allowed to discourage people from challenging discrimination and oppression or stigmatize them for doing so. Sadly, issues relating to transgender or gender-fluid people have been a major and vitriolic target of 'anti-woke' prejudice.

Promoting equality

Without doubt, the equality, diversity and inclusion movement has had a huge impact at one level upon all aspects of UK society. Organizations are now commonly required to have equality, diversity and inclusion policies; no one should be discriminated against on the grounds of age, sex, gender identity, religion, political affiliation, sexual orientation, disability and so on. In this sense it now represents the 'norm', in terms of expectations at least, if not actual outcomes (see Chapter 16 for a discussion of how this is starting to change).

The importance of the concept of equality is emphasized by Thompson (2018a, p. xvii) who argues that

> contemporary western societies are characterized by inequality. ... For those of us involved in working with people and their problems, this represents a fundamental challenge, in so far as decisions made and actions taken can play a significant role in either moving towards a greater degree of equality or reinforcing existing inequalities.

This highlights the ways in which our professional and/or managerial interactions with people will be rendered ineffective, if not positively dangerous, if we do not take account of the power dynamics between the worker or manager and those who become involved with them in a professional relationship. These are issues to which we must return later in this chapter when exploring anti-discriminatory practice. For the moment, we need to focus on ways in which the equality, diversity and inclusion movement sought to ensure that all citizens would receive equal treatment across all aspects of society. This has been an important expression of the value base being explored in this chapter.

However, in their Foreword to a helpful introduction to these issues Amos and Ouseley (in Cheung-Judge and Henley, 1994, p. xi) offered a warning:

> The 1990s has been characterized as the decade of equal opportunities in Britain, and yet the reality of the experience of many women and ethnic

minorities in Britain is of a society that has not delivered equality despite the existence of race relations and sex discrimination legislation. It often seems as if nothing has changed.

They are highlighting the danger of rhetoric being mistaken for reality, where the opportunities available to minority groups, for example, can be kept to a minimum by a clever manipulation of power and influence, whatever the equality policies might say. Important though this caveat is, however, it would be foolish to underestimate the impact of equality in the story of the values debate.

The story has been told in much detail elsewhere, but the main themes deserve brief mention, because they illustrate both the values issues, and also some of the power dynamics highlighted by Thompson (2018a) in his influential text.

In the post-war period in Britain, some major social changes became perhaps inevitable. With many men away in the armed forces, women began to play a more prominent role, demonstrating that they were every bit as capable as men in performing a wide range of activities. No wonder that, with an awakened self-confidence, they were not simply going to 'roll over' once the war was over, and let men resume where they had left off in the social order.

Other changes had a profound impact. Men who had been seriously injured in the war found that peacetime proved to be, if anything, even more daunting. Society valued strength and the capacity to get things done; it offered little opportunity for wounded and disabled people to fulfil a useful role in society. The move from 'war hero' to 'useless burden' (hero to zero) was for some a very sudden and painful transition. In such soil the seeds of promoting equality were sown and quickly blossomed. Disabled people began to demand their rights to gainful employment; women no longer adopted subservient roles. Later on, the full implications of how black people were being treated hit home, and the doors of employment and housing were prised open in a way that would have shocked pre-war society.

In some ways this story can be charted by a series of key legislative changes. The Disabled Persons (Employment) Act started things moving in 1944. The first Race Relations Act was passed in 1965. This was only a start, of course; each of these needed radical improvements. The final destination of true equality enshrined in legislation still proves elusive, as critics of current disability and immigration legislation, to cite but two examples, demonstrate. Nevertheless, it is always important to take the first step towards change, and these Acts, together with subsequent Equal Pay Acts (1970, amended 1983); Sex Discrimination Act (1975, amended 1986), marked a trend towards implementing the fundamental value base of equality.

This development illustrates very well Thompson's point that, at the heart of these issues is power, and that if the discriminatory and oppressive influences on people's lives were going to be altered, then powerful steps had to be taken in order to effect significant change. In fact, that same critique can be applied to all the changes that occurred during the last decades of the twentieth century and the early years of the twenty-first century. There has been a constant tension between those who are seeking to achieve a more just and equal society and those who are determined to maintain their privilege and the status quo. And, whatever the nature or source of the critique, the underlying issues remain: the extent to which the values of equality are taken seriously and put into effect, and the impact of power upon those processes.

Although the legal basis of positive changes is noteworthy, we should not limit our understanding to legal matters. As Thompson (2021) emphasizes, practices that are limited to legal compliance would not be truly anti-discriminatory. A much broader, values-based approach is called for, as the law is a fairly blunt instrument and, indeed, not all forms of discrimination are illegal.

These issues are important to note in the values debate because they high-light the wider societal and political contexts that both reflect and often shape our values, and the quality of life that people do, or do not enjoy. It is this context that is of such fundamental importance to an understanding of contemporary practice, and which has led to the development of the major approach that has come to be known as anti-discriminatory practice. No introductory discussion about the context of the values debate would be complete without a brief exploration of this key theme, and so we shall shortly be focusing our attention it. However, we first want to comment on the use of the term 'equality'.

A note on equality

This term has caused a lot of confusion over the years. In its literal sense, it can mean sameness, as it is used in mathematics – for example, in saying $2 + 2 = 4$, we are saying that 2 plus 2 is the same as four. However, it can also mean balanced, rather than the same and thus, by extension, refer to fairness. When, for example, we say that men and women are (or should be) equal, we are not saying they are the same, as clearly there are significant biological and social differences between men and women. Rather, what is meant by equality in that sense is not that there is no difference between men and women, but that there are no legitimate ground for treating one gender less fairly or less favourably than another.

Sadly, the tendency to interpret equality to mean sameness has discouraged some people from being involved in efforts to promote equality, as they have no wish to disregard the differences between men and women (or between gay and straight people, or Christians and Muslims and so on). Indeed, the idea of diversity as a value is about valuing or even celebrating differences. It is therefore essential that we move away from the idea that promoting equality means treating everybody the same – it is about treating everybody fairly and not allowing differences to serve as the basis of unfair discrimination. Equality, then, when used in its moral, professional and political sense – rather than its mathematical sense – should be interpreted as fairness, a lack of discrimination.

In recent years, some people have followed the American lead in using the term 'equity' in place of equality in order to highlight that it is not about sameness and a lack of diversity. Whether we use equity or equality, the key point is that it is fundamentally about fairness, about social justice.

Anti-discriminatory practice

Although to social workers and some other professionals the concept of anti-discriminatory practice will appear familiar, to others it may be less so. To a few, it may appear to be a puzzling, even a jargonistic concept. It is important therefore to contextualize what we would argue is a key basis of practice that must underpin the work of any helping professional. At its simplest, anti-discriminatory practice may be regarded as a practical expression of the value base that is being explored in this manual. If each and every individual is regarded as unique and special, then how might this 'value base' find expression in professional practice?

Part of the response is that each professional worker or manager – no matter what area of practice they operate in – must ensure that, in what they say and how they behave, they are doing everything in their power to ensure that the individual 'on the receiving end' – whether client or colleague – feels that they are being treated with dignity, respect and honesty. Anything less than that would be a denial of the value base they claim to espouse.

So far, this would attract little critical comment: it is perhaps a statement of the obvious as far as contemporary professional practice is concerned – not that we should become blasé about this, of course. This 'gold standard' of 'best practice' remains both an ideal and a challenge to every worker, and there are myriad examples where people are left feeling undervalued by their workers, managers or helpers.

Where anti-discriminatory practice comes into its own, however, is the way in which it seeks to enable professional helpers, workers and managers to begin to address the wider context in which the individual is located. We have already begun to explore in the discussion about the great 'isms' earlier in this chapter the complex nature of discrimination and oppression, and the ways in which people's lives and life chances can be seriously curtailed by their social circumstances. If such circumstances were to be ignored, no matter how sensitively a worker deals with an individual in need, the root causes of the difficulties would not be resolved, and the best that could be achieved is a sensitively placed sticking plaster that inevitably will come off very quickly once it is exposed to the searching waters of discrimination and oppression.

Anti-discriminatory practice therefore seeks to act upon the implications of this wider understanding and appreciation of how society functions, hence Thompson's use of PCS analysis, as discussed earlier. One of the points Thompson's work emphasizes is that most discrimination is unintentional. For example, for every deliberate act of racism or sexism, there will be many more that are unintentional (but none the less problematic and unacceptable) instances based in the unwitting reliance on stereotypes, use of biased processes or procedures, inbuilt system biases or other such ways of producing unequal and unfair outcomes.

A good example of this wider understanding working in practice may be seen in the work of Citizens Advice that is rightly renowned for the ways in which it gives free, confidential and impartial advice to anyone who needs it. At an individual level this can be life-changing and life-enhancing help, as a planned package for handling acute debt is worked out in partnership between adviser and caller. But alongside all of this vital individual work, there is the social policy arm to the organization's work, where at local, regional or national levels issues are identified that are having a negative impact upon the people who come to them for help. As these issues are identified, so pressure and influence can be brought to bear upon local or national government to make changes to the 'system'. Governments may or may not take heed when such matters are brought to their attention, of course.

Key point

When it comes to discrimination and oppression, the issues need to be understood at a far wider level and not be restricted to the personal level. Changes at wider levels will affect not only those individuals who have presented their problems in the first place, but also the population as a whole.

It is at this point that the term 'emancipatory practice' can be usefully brought back into the discussion. As the name suggests, there is an element of being 'set free' inherent in this term. If radical solutions can be found to the difficulties individuals face that address these wider perspectives, then there is a chance of more long-lasting solutions being found, rather than short-term cosmetic approaches that only deal with the symptoms. Best practice – which means anti-discriminatory practice dealing with issues of discrimination and oppression as well as the individualized effect of these large-scale issues – will have an emancipatory impact upon people, as their life chances are enhanced and enriched.

This is not to suggest for a moment that these objectives can be easily achieved – far from it. The great 'isms' are far too entrenched for such naïve optimism. But anti-discriminatory practice is so important because it takes these issues with the utmost seriousness, and factors them into the help and support that workers give to individuals they are working with.

TIP! Try and make sure you get the balance right. Don't be naïve about easy answers, but don't assume that nothing can be done. We can all play an important role in tackling discrimination and oppression.

One final point to note about anti-discriminatory practice for now is to clarify the relationship between discrimination and oppression. This is another issue where the use of terminology has caused much confusion. As we see it, discrimination is the process (or set of processes) whereby people (individuals, groups, communities or categories of people) are treated less favourably because they are – or are perceived to be – different in one or more ways. The result of discrimination is very often oppression – that is, the treatment of people in unfair and inhumane ways and very much to their detriment.

We therefore see discrimination as the *process* and oppression as the *outcome*. So, in our way of thinking, whether we use the term anti-discriminatory practice or anti-oppressive practice, we are basically talking about the same thing, namely *emancipatory* practice.

Values-based practice

We bring this chapter to a close by reflecting on important developments that have happened in other spheres of people work. If it is true that the theme of anti-discriminatory practice has had social work as a pioneer and field leader in exploring the relevance and implications for best people work practice, then it is also true to say that, within health services there has been an equally important development in recent years that has placed values-based practice centre stage for a wide cross-section of health professionals.

The work of Woodbridge and Fulford (2004) focuses on what they call values-based practice in mental health care, but it has wider implications for people work in other fields too. In many ways the issues and dilemmas facing health workers are similar to those in other professions, as an example of the comments of a community psychiatric nurse from their workbook illustrates:

> I am constantly working in an environment of lots of people's different values and trying to make sense of that. For example, I'm working with someone who is using our services who has very different values to me; not only that, but his values are very different to his parents'. I'm juggling with these values, struggling to tease out the issues and bring some clarity to my own thinking.
>
> (p. 7)

In short, the values workbook aims

> to provide a framework for the analysis of values in practice … A framework … to enable people to work in a respectful and sensitive way with different values and perspectives present in practice.
>
> (p. 7)

The workbook is based on a substantial amount of work done by the authors who offer a definition of values-based practice as: 'the theory and skills base for effective health care decision-making where different (and hence potentially conflicting) values are in play' (p. 16). This definition, although aimed at health professionals, has much to commend it for our later discussions that will apply to a much wider range of human services workers. It is likely that anyone, from whatever people work perspective, will immediately be able to relate to that definition. It captures many of the dilemmas about working with people that at times bewilder and perplex us as professionals, but which at the same time provide some of the challenge and enrichment of people work in all its many-faceted themes.

Conclusion

We have introduced you to the important underlying themes and issues that underpin the value base of our work and have explored some of the ideas and approaches you need to understand. All this has been a preparation for the discussion on how all this impinges upon actual practice. We hope that already you have begun to make some links with the work you currently are undertaking or expect to become involved with if you are currently a student about to go out into a work-based setting as part of your training. There is always a danger that 'theory' and 'practice' are regarded as two separate, almost mutually exclusive concepts. Students, for example, who go out into their practice-based settings, having completed part of the academic requirements of their course, sometimes have older, 'wiser' people say to them: 'Welcome to the real world – this is how you will have to do things now'. The implication is clear: whatever they have learned in their so-called ivory towers, the sharp realities of practice mean that a more hard-headed pragmatic approach has to be adopted.

Our view, however, is that values are just as hard at work in a hard-nosed pragmatic approach as they are anywhere else. We need to be aware of how our personal and professional values affect our daily practice, no matter how overstretched the service we seek to provide may have become. Far from being separated from practice, the issues we have been reflecting upon are the fundamental bedrock for how we can practise safely and effectively on a day-to-day basis.

Exercise 2

What do you see as the main values underpinning your work within your particular profession? For each one state why you think it is important and what adverse consequences could arise from its absence in actual practice situations.

Confidentiality

Introduction

In Chapter 2 we discussed the topic of 'making sense of values' at some length. This is because, in many ways, the understanding it offers acts as a foundation for the issues we are going to be discussing in the remaining chapters. Not least among these other issues is confidentiality, and so that is our subject matter for Chapter 3.

Why is confidentiality important?

Because we work with information received from clients or from other sources, the way in which we deal with it will have major implications for our relationships with the people we serve. That is, if information is used carelessly or inappropriately clients are likely to have little trust in, or respect for, workers. They may feel betrayed, used and devalued – not worthy of the privacy and respect they would normally expect to enjoy. Failing to handle information carefully, sensitively and appropriately can therefore have very damaging consequences. It follows, then, that it is important for us to be clear about the DOs and DON'Ts of information, so that we can be sure that a lack of confidentiality does not cause problems for our clients, ourselves and our employers. Confidentiality is a fundamental value of people work, and so we run the risk of things going badly wrong if we do not take full account of these important issues of confidentiality. To help you with this, this chapter looks at some of the key questions that arise in relation to confidentiality. The first one to be tackled is perhaps the most basic one: What exactly do we mean by confidentiality?

DOI: 10.4324/9781003689614-4

What is confidentiality?

Biestek (1961, p. 121) defined confidentiality as

> the preservation of secret information concerning the client that is disclosed in the professional relationship. Confidentiality is based upon a basic right of the client; it is an ethical obligation of the case worker and is necessary for effective casework service. The client's right, however, is not absolute. Moreover, the client's secret is often shared with other professional persons within the agency and in other agencies; the obligation then binds all equally.

Biestek was referring to casework, the traditional approach to social work, but the same points can be seen to apply also to social care. Let us now look, in a little more detail, at each of these in turn.

1. Secret information
    Confidential information is, by definition, secret information; it is not intended to be generally available. This raises the question of boundaries – where do you draw the line between who should know and who should not? – an important point to which we shall return below.
2. A basic right
    Like all citizens, people in need of professional support have certain basic rights and we need to recognize confidentiality as a primary one amongst these. It is important for people's dignity, self-respect and self-esteem.
3. Not an absolute right
    However, in some circumstances, the right to confidentiality may need to be overruled – for example, for legal reasons or the protection of others. Once again, we shall discuss this further under the heading of 'boundaries'.
4. Shared information
    As professionals, we mostly operate on behalf of an employing agency. Information is therefore confidential not to you as an individual, but to your agency – for example, in terms of written records. This can sometimes lead to conflicts and dilemmas.
5. Equal obligation
    When confidential information is shared within an organization or between agencies, it remains none the less confidential. The fact that it has been shared to some degree does not mean that it can be shared further – what *is* shared is the obligation to maintain confidentiality.

TIP! Make sure that you know what your employer's policy on confidentiality is. If there is no formal policy, it is wise to clarify what expectations of you your employers have (with regard to confidentiality).

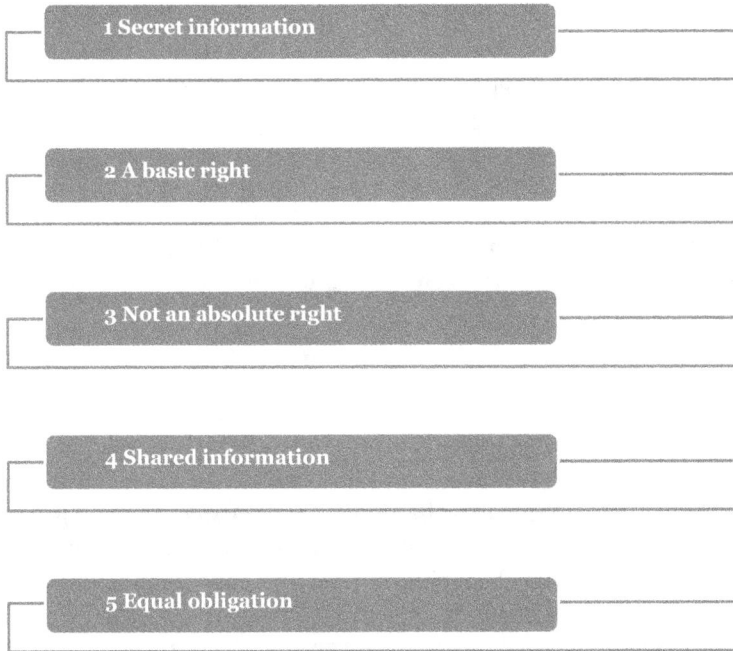

Figure 3.1 Dimensions of confidentiality

If you work with children: Do you know where a copy of the safeguarding or child protection procedures are and what your obligations are under these? If you work with adults: Are there policies or procedures relating to the protection of adults that apply to you? Do you know what your obligations are?

Boundaries

A boundary is a dividing line or limit. Boundaries are therefore an important aspect of confidentiality – they raise the key question of: Where do you draw the line? This can be seen to apply in a number of ways. Let's consider each of these in turn.

Who should know?

Where do we draw the line between who should know and who should not? To answer this question, you will need to consider:

- The nature of the information given;
- The wishes of the person giving the information;

- Your employer's policy on confidentiality and storage of information;
- Legal requirements;
- Other requirements – for example, safeguarding procedures.

What needs to be recorded?

Obviously, not all information given by clients can or should be entered in written records. So, how do we decide what gets written down and what does not? There is no simple or straightforward answer to this question, and so we shall look at it in more detail below.

When should confidentiality be overridden?

Confidentiality is a right and, as such, it can only be overridden in exceptional circumstances. The general principle will be discussed below under the heading of 'Rights and Choice'. However, as confidentiality is such a thorny issue, it is worth devoting some time to these issues here. The key word is that of protection, whether the protection of the individual concerned or the protection of others. A helpful way of understanding this is to regard information given in confidence as sacrosanct unless and until this comes into conflict with your duty to safeguard the health and wellbeing of those in your care, your colleagues and others, including the community at large. Examples of such conflict would be:

- *Suicide risk* – This type of information must be passed on, even though this may create a moral dilemma for you if the person concerned asks you to keep the information to yourself;
- *Risk to others* – This covers a wide range of possibilities and includes risk of infection or an intention to harm someone else;
- *Safeguarding procedures* – Child protection procedures have been in existence for many years, and official procedures now generally include the protection of other vulnerable groups at risk of abuse. It is essential that you are aware of your obligations under the appropriate procedures and that you abide by them.

If you should find yourself in a situation where such a conflict applies, it is important that you do not carry the responsibility for the problem on your own. Make sure you discuss the situation with your line manager or another senior colleague. If you do not, you could find yourself not only in a stressful dilemma but also, quite possibly, in a situation where you are being held partly responsible for a harmful outcome or even subject to a disciplinary charge.

Official records

It is, of course, common practice for organizations to keep official records, whether in manual files, on computer, or both. Such records have important implications for confidentiality in terms of:

1. What is kept on record and for how long;
2. Who has access to such records in normal circumstances;
3. Who else has access to the records in exceptional circumstances;
4. Whether the records are securely stored.

1. What is kept on record and for how long will depend largely on the policy and established practices of your employers. It is therefore important that you make sure that you have a clear understanding of what is expected of you as far as written records are concerned. In particular, a very important question to ask is: What sort of things have to be put on record? Some types of information may have to be recorded even if you were asked to keep the information secret. The point to note here is that the information you receive is received on behalf of the organization you work for. That is, the information given belongs not to you personally, but to your employing organization.
2. To maintain confidentiality, we have to be clear about who is allowed to have access to records. It is then the responsibility of staff to ensure that unauthorized persons do not have access to confidential information. Care therefore needs to be taken to make sure that records are not left lying around or allowed to get into the hands of the wrong people.
3. At certain times, other people may have a right to see the information kept on record. Examples of this would be formal inquiries or investigations, or court cases. Complaints and representation procedures may well result in wider access to records by senior staff or independent arbiters.
4. There is, of course, little point in trying to maintain confidentiality if records are not securely kept. Are written records kept under lock and key? Are computer records protected from unauthorized access? These are important and significant questions – as indeed, are the key questions of: 'What part do I play in keeping confidential records secure? "and" What are my responsibilities in safeguarding confidentiality?'

How we deal with records in particular and confidentiality in general will depend, to a large extent, on the policies and expectations of our employers. These, in turn, will largely depend on legal requirements and guidelines. Space does not permit a detailed exploration of the legal framework of confidentiality, but your employer should be able to give you access to suitable guidance and/or training.

Reflective moment

How would you feel if an organization that held sensitive information about you were to be lax and allow unauthorized people to have sight of that information?

Guidelines for good practice

As we have seen, confidentiality is a complex subject and one that can cause a number of problems if it is not handled carefully and sensitively. This manual cannot ensure that you do not encounter any of these problems, but the guidance we give here can, we hope, help you to minimize the chances of things going wrong. We therefore offer the following guidelines as helpful suggestions for dealing with the thorny issues of confidentiality.

1 Be clear about your responsibilities

As we have noted, confidentiality is a complex and thorny matter and so it is not too difficult to become confused and lose track of the issues. When this happens, it is then quite easy for confidentiality to be breached inadvertently. Confidential information can so easily 'slip out' inappropriately, with potentially disastrous results. It is therefore imperative that you are clear about your responsibilities with regard to confidentiality, that you take them seriously and that you are vigilant.

2 Inform clients of where they stand

As confidentiality is not an absolute right, you will need to make sure that clients (and others who may give you information in confidence) are dear about:

- Where and how information will be stored;
- Who will have access to it;
- In what circumstances confidentiality will be overridden and with what consequences;
- What rights the individual has with regard to obtaining access to the information stored.

It is helpful if these matters can be clarified sooner rather than later. If not, you run the risk of creating a very difficult situation in which people feel you have misled them or hidden things from them. Clearly, this makes working on the basis of trust a very difficult undertaking.

3 Obtain proof of identity when necessary

It is possible for confidential information to 'fall into the wrong hands' if we are lax in passing on information. For example, if we do not check the identity of people requesting information, we may be guilty of passing on that information to people who have no right to it. We are under an obligation to maintain confidentiality and so it is important to seek proof of identity whenever there is any doubt. If, for example, someone makes a telephone enquiry, it may be necessary to ask for their number and ring them back, having first checked that it is a bona fide number for the agency concerned.

4 Don't be afraid to ask for help

Dealing with the potential conflicts and dilemmas of confidentiality is a demanding task and one that can give rise to a lot of worry and pressure. This being the case, it is important that you know where to get advice and support. But, just knowing where to get help is not enough – you've got to actually use that help when you need to. Asking for help is not a sign of weakness. Rather, it is a sign of professional commitment to working together to provide the best care for your clients.

5 Try to create an atmosphere of trust

The importance of maintaining confidentiality can become just a hollow phrase if there is no atmosphere of trust in which people feel able to talk about personal and private matters, to discuss their worries and concerns. Without this atmosphere of trust, people can feel lonely, isolated and unsupported. In this way, extra barriers and tensions are created which, in turn, create additional pressures and problems for service users and staff alike. Of course, generating an atmosphere of trust is no easy or straightforward matter. But, one thing that can make a significant contribution is, ironically, maintaining confidentiality. Trust and confidentiality

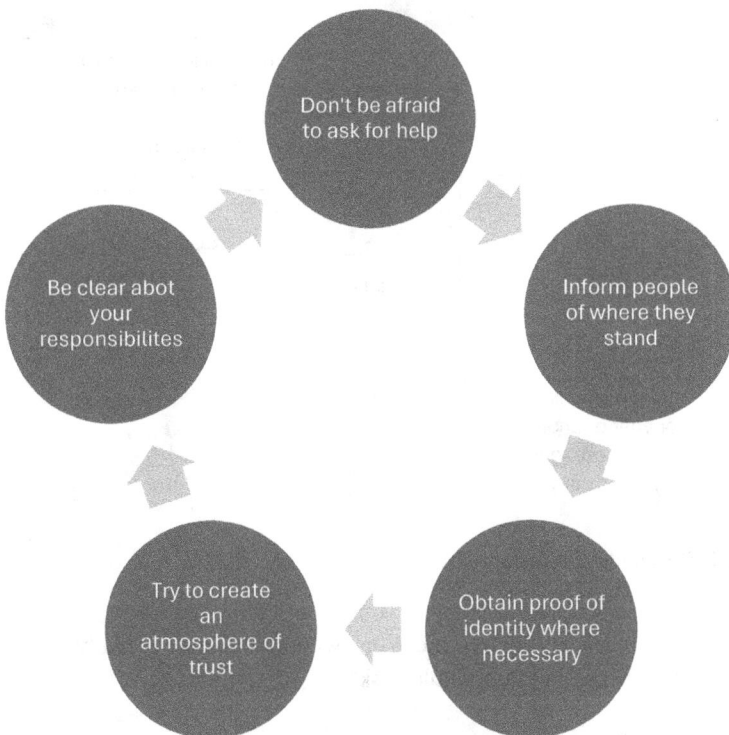

Figure 3.2 Managing confidentiality

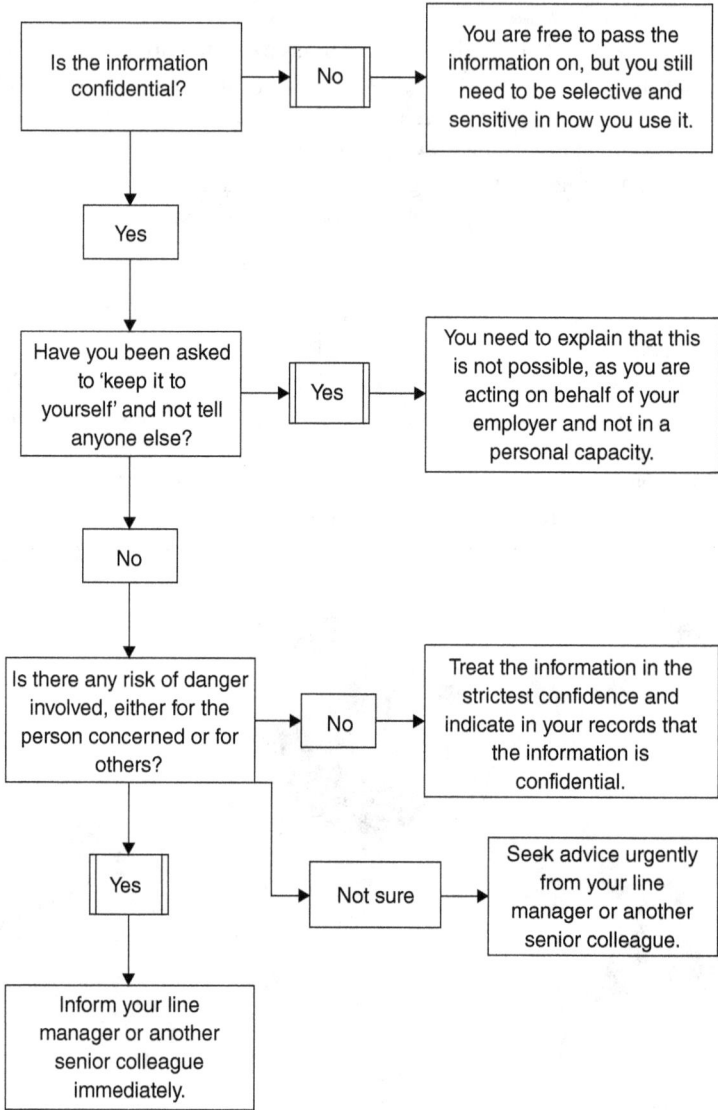

Figure 3.3 Confidentiality flow diagram

reinforce each other. Trying to achieve one without the other is likely to prove an extremely difficult, if not impossible, task.

Conclusion

Working in the people professions often means dealing with vulnerable people at a personal level. This makes your job a very important and responsible one – and one that can easily go sadly wrong if we are not careful. Confidentiality is therefore very significant in this respect. If it is handled well, it plays an important part in ensuring high-quality practice. But, if it is not handled, we can cause major problems, leaving people feeling betrayed, unsupported and undervalued. We very much hope that this too can help you to make sure, as far as possible, that the outcomes you achieve are positive ones.

Exercise 3

Consider each of the three exceptional circumstances where confidentiality can be overridden and answer the questions that follow:

Suicide risk
What would you regard as indicators of possible suicidal intention? Who would you inform if you encountered such indicators?

Risk to others
What would you regard as indicators of possible harm to others? Who would you inform if you encountered such indicators?

Safeguarding
What would you regard as indicators of possible abuse? Who would you inform if you encountered such indicators?

Tackling discrimination and oppression

Introduction

Chapter 2 encouraged you to reflect on some of the complex issues that seriously undermine and diminish the life experiences of many citizens. These have been summed up in the key concept of oppression. The value base of social work and other human services stresses the importance of recognizing and challenging oppression wherever it is encountered: this is now fundamental to much professional practice.

This chapter seeks to give you some examples of how all of this might work in practice. Before moving on to this, however, it is important to explore a little further our perspective on all of this.

The struggle for social justice

In Greek mythology, there is the story of Sisyphus whose life task was to push an enormous boulder up a very steep hill. No sooner was he within sight of the summit than the sheer weight of the boulder got the better of him and the next thing he knew he was down at the bottom once more, the challenging task needing to be begun all over again. To his credit, he never gave up, presumably because the task itself was judged to be sufficiently important that it deserved his continuous effort.

This image will ring bells, for sure, with anyone who has begun seriously to grapple with the issues of anti-discriminatory practice and its efforts to address the oppression that discrimination gives rise to: it will certainly ring true for anyone

DOI: 10.4324/9781003689614-5

who has been on the receiving end of oppressive behaviour, and who knows what it is like to live in a society that is discriminatory towards people who are different in one or more ways. It does sometimes feel that, for all the progress that has been made with legislation and education, for example, we fall back down the hill when another racial murder or assault takes place, or when heterosexist attitudes reassert themselves on a national scale to take just two examples. It would be foolish in the extreme to suggest that the task of achieving equality, and of putting anti-discriminatory values into practice, is anything but a struggle, sometimes of Sisyphean proportions.

Celebrating diversity

Having said that, there is another image that sustains many people involved in these issues that is best summed up in the word 'celebration'. Fortunately, there are many examples throughout the country where people from a wide range of backgrounds come together simply to celebrate. The famous Notting Hill carnival in London is but one example of many where celebration comes to the fore and people simply enjoy each other's company as they glimpse what society could be like.

This image of celebration is not to suggest that life is, or could be, one long party, but it does put us in touch with the vision we have for our society, and you cannot have a vision without it having a value base.

Tied in with this is another phrase you will encounter in some of the more recent literature on the values debate, and that is emancipatory practice. Put at its simplest, this means getting rid of all the barriers and obstacles that get in the way of people enjoying themselves and each other as members of society. Thompson (2018a, p. 58) expresses it more comprehensively:

Emancipatory practice involves helping to set people free from:

- discriminatory attitudes, values, actions and cultural assumptions;
- structures of inequality and oppression, both within organizations and in the social order more broadly;
- the barriers of bad faith and alienation that stand in the way of empowerment and self-direction;
- powerful ideological and other social forces that limit opportunities and maintain the status quo;
- traditional practices which, although often based on good intentions, have the effect of maintaining inequalities and halting progress towards more appropriate forms of practice.

Underlying this statement is a vision of what society could be like, and the role that human services professionals can play in helping this to be achieved. It is this vision of a society where people accept and celebrate the diversity of all its members.

Such large-scale values, however, seem a long way away from the everyday practice dilemmas encountered by managers and practitioners who frequently remind people that they have to work 'in the real world'. This realism must not be dismissed, of course, but underneath it there so often lies a sense of defeatism and acquiescence to the 'status quo', as if to say that 'there is nothing any of us can do about these large issues, so why bother? Let's simply do what we can as best we can, and leave it at that; after all, there is a very tight budget'. As we seek to grapple with these issues, unless we are part of the solution, we shall remain part of the problem.

Before we move on to consider some specific examples, it is worth briefly approaching the issue from the other direction, namely your own personal experience. No one writing a manual like this can possibly know who will be reading it, and what experiences have brought them to the point of considering a career in the people professions. Therefore, the material that follows may or may not reflect your own situation, but we invite you to use it as imaginatively as possible.

Questions to ask yourself:

- If you are a woman, how do you feel you are treated by men generally?
- Are there ways in which you feel put down or devalued?
- If you are disabled, do you feel that you are valued for who you are, or are you sometimes made to feel a second-class citizen because of your disability?
- If you are black, or Asian, or from another minority ethnic group, do you feel you are valued and made to feel that there is a contribution you can make to the community?
- If you are a white male, do you sometimes feel that everyone is blaming you for the ills of society over which you feel you have no control?
- If you are part of the LGBTQ+ community, are there people or groups of people you would be anxious or afraid to disclose this to?
- If a member of your family has been to prison, or is misusing drugs, do other people make you feel somehow to blame?
- If you have experienced unemployment, or acute financial hardship, have you been made to feel that it is all your fault?
- If you have experienced mental health problems, do you think that people now treat you differently?
- If you come from a working-class background, do other people sometimes regard you as inferior?
- If you are Deaf or hard of hearing or have sight difficulties, do you find that some people simply ignore you?

This list is obviously not exhaustive – your own experiences may be quite different from those we have selected as examples, in which case please spend a few moments before moving on, identifying the ways in which you feel you may have been discriminated against.

These examples are located in your ordinary everyday experiences; they demonstrate ways in which you have been treated unfairly; ways in which other people have not celebrated the contribution you have to make to our society. You know how that feels; you also know how you would like to be treated, and how things might be different if you were fully accepted, and if your contribution to society was recognized, valued and celebrated. That, quite simply, is how we would like the people we work with to feel as a result of our intervention and our commitment to emancipatory practice.

The last paragraph ended with a bold sweeping statement. When you read it, you may have reacted by feeling 'that's all very well, but …'. Please make a note of any points you would like to make in response, and which you would like to explore and discuss further.

The notes you make will be important points to bear in mind as you work through the examples from practice given below. These ('this is all very well, but … ') notes are, if you like, a further dimension to the important process of locating yourself, and recognizing where you are coming from. This is especially important because the personality (and humanity) of the worker in the end is the most important tool of the trade in the work we do. Our values, our attitudes and our commitment to good practice will come across powerfully to everyone we deal with. If, deep down, we despise some people, and feel unable to celebrate the contribution they can make to society, that too will come across, whether we like it or not.

TIP! This is not the same, however, as saying we should approve of, or condone, all behaviours. The law and our own professional values that stand firm against all forms of oppressive, abusive and exploitative behaviour make that very clear.

We hope that, among the comments you listed, was the objection to any attempt to explore the issues of oppression and discrimination in separate, unconnected ways. It's all very well identifying certain strands in society and illustrating them separately by showing how issues of race, gender, class, age, disability and sexuality, for example, affect people's lives. The reality can be far more complex, and many people are affected by several aspects of oppression at the same time. This brings into the discussion the concept of multiple oppression or 'intersectionality', and the importance of understanding how this can severely disadvantage people, both individually and collectively.

It is not a question of having a 'values template' that we can place upon a particular situation presented to us and hope that this will produce a clear way forward. Instead, we are in difficult terrain where we are not sure exactly how multiple oppressions will have an impact upon a particular person and their circumstances. The process of discovery, therefore, is crucial: it makes the process of assessment all the more important.

Countering discrimination and oppression: Some examples from practice

The case studies that follow are designed to give you an opportunity to explore the relationship between values issues and actual practice. They are intended to provoke discussion and are perhaps best used in small groups once you have undertaken the preliminary work by yourself. The first one is followed by some commentary to help you get launched, but we encourage you to spend some time on the others working by yourself to see what issues emerge. We have left some space for you to make notes about the values issues that arise and how you might possibly deal with them.

Case study 1

John is a white male social worker in an adult services team in an inner-city area.

He is 26 years old and has been working in this team for about two months. He is called to Springtime residential home because the staff are concerned about the wellbeing of Mrs Khan, who was placed there by John's predecessor about four months ago. Mrs Khan is 86 years old and was placed in Springtime after she was discovered lying on the floor of her house, having collapsed and broken her arm. A preliminary investigation suggested that she was not able to look after herself, and immediate residential respite care was organized. Shortly after this, however, the social worker involved went off sick with a stress-related illness, and the case was not reallocated due to pressure of other work within the team.

When he visited Springtime, John was dismayed to hear the full story. Mrs Khan stayed in her room all day; she hardly ate any of the food brought to her; she had no visitors. She was taken down to the residents' lounge but, as no one could understand her, she simply sat there gazing into space. Her arm had begun to heal well, but she still kept it in a sling. The staff were adamant that the social worker had to make Mrs Khan fit in to their regime. Many of the staff spoke to Mrs Khan in a loud voice, hoping to make her understand.

JOHN'S RESPONSE

John's initial response was a mild panic. He was not comfortable dealing with older people and had hardly any experience of working with Asian elders. He felt under enormous pressure from the staff at Springtime to do something quickly, and to regard the problem as being Mrs Khan. He felt uneasy about the attitude of the staff but decided to spend his initial visit gathering as much relevant information as possible. He returned to the office to consult with colleagues and his manager. Among the issues they identified were:

- How comprehensive had the assessment on Mrs Khan been originally? Had it taken into account her various needs, including appropriate diet; cultural needs; links with her own community; communication issues?
- How well (if at all) was Springtime equipped to provide care in a multicultural community?
- To what extent were Mrs Khan's own wishes taken into account? Did anyone know what these were? Had anyone tried to find out?
- To what extent was Springtime encouraging residents to take at least some responsibility for their own welfare?
- Were there grounds for complaint about Springtime's regime and standard of care?

John was aware that some Asian elders are lonely and neglected, and that the view that all Asian families look after their own is an inaccurate stereotype. He was nevertheless anxious to discover whether Mrs Khan did have any family members nearby and, if so, why there had not been any contact. John sought out an official interpreter who was female and fluent in several Asian languages. He returned to Springtime, and within 20 minutes Mrs Khan seemed a different person. She poured out her sad story to the interpreter. There had been a family argument recently and, as a result, she had been ostracized; no one had been near her home for about six months.

Springtime was comfortable enough, but she could not make herself understood; her dietary needs were ignored, and she felt she was pining to death. She wanted to return to her own home if at all possible. Over the next couple of weeks, a more detailed assessment was carried out and a package of care was negotiated to enable Mrs Khan to return home. She was put in touch with a support worker who was fluent in her own language and her GP was fully updated. With the agreement of his manager, and with the interpreter's help, John responded to Mrs Khan's request to contact her family; he composed a letter to them, explaining what had happened and informing them that she had now returned home.

John submitted a report to his manager about Springtime, recommending that it be inspected and that, as an absolute minimum, the staff be given training in cultural awareness and how to meet the needs of a wide cross-section of the community that, as a registered care home, they were required to do.

John also asked his manager to review the case allocation system that he felt was at fault in allowing Mrs Khan's case to remain unallocated following his predecessor's departure on sick leave.

In reflecting on this piece of work, John was able to identify several aspects of discriminatory practice, including racism (both personal and institutional); ageism; absence of any partnership working or empowerment: institutionalization, leading to learned helplessness among the residents. He was also able to see where individual practice could make a difference, and where he needed to explore wider institutional approaches.

Are there any other issues you feel are important in this story? Please make a note of them.

Case study 2

Janine is a black female worker (aged 35) in an adult services team. She has some shared responsibility with two other colleagues for a local hostel that often takes people with mental health difficulties. She is asked to go to see one of the residents, Michael, who has become more and more isolated over recent weeks. He plays loud music late at night, causing upset to other residents and the neighbours. The staff suspect he is not taking his medication and fear that he will become violent. They have asked Janine to help because, like Michael, she is black and will therefore be able to understand and do something.

Case study 3

Becky is a single parent with three young children, aged 4, 2 and 1. She is white, aged 23. She has found it increasingly difficult to cope both emotionally and financially over recent months, and has run up several debts, including the gas, electricity and rent. She has not been paying her fines (for not having a TV licence). She earns some extra money occasionally through prostitution, when she gets her friend to babysit. In desperation, she approaches her local council for help, especially with her financial problems. When a worker (female, aged 55) visits her at her flat, Becky is dismayed when she is told that she had better give up smoking so much, and start pulling her socks up as a mother, or she will find that her children get taken off her and put into care.

Case study 4

Anton lives with his wife and five children, with six other families on one of the sites reserved for travelling families on the outskirts of a large city. The facilities are generally felt to be adequate and the local community, by and large, leaves them alone to get on with their own way of life. All five of Anton's children have begun to attend local schools since their arrival in the area two months ago. Four of them are settling in well, but Sylvia, who is now 14, says that she doesn't need to go to school anymore because Romany tradition says it is not necessary. The education welfare officer is alerted to Sylvia's poor school attendance record and visits the family at home.

Case study 5

Sala (21, an Asian male) comes to the local council office to complain that the neighbours are making life intolerable for him and his partner (Barry, 20). The neighbours complain that he and Barry play music late at night and they have also put offensive notes through their letter box. Sala feels that the complaints about noise are not justified, as they never play music after 11.30 pm which the neighbours often do, especially at weekends. He says that he and Barry keep themselves to themselves and simply want to be allowed to get on with their lives in peace. Things have become intolerable recently, however, and they want to move to another part of the town. Their flat is damp and the council have not responded to their requests for repairs to be done. They ask for social work help in supporting their application to the council for an exchange of flats.

Case study 6

Kevin is 24, black and single. He lives in a local authority flat and is on state benefits. He has managed to find several casual labouring jobs over recent years, but his attempts to find more permanent work have so far been unsuccessful. He went out with a group of white friends to celebrate his birthday in a local night club two months ago. They were sitting quietly in a corner enjoying a drink and watching the cabaret when a fight broke out close to them. The police arrived very quickly, and to his horror, the police included Kevin with the group who were fighting, and he was arrested for causing criminal damage and disturbing the peace. In spite of legal assistance, he was found guilty at court and ordered to pay a fine. Since then, he has become increasingly depressed; he stays indoors a lot of the time and has given up all attempts at finding work. He has just received a letter from the Job Centre, however, saying that his entitlement to benefit is soon to expire. In desperation, he seeks social work help, asking them to support his case for continuing on benefits because of his mental health problems.

Countering discrimination and oppression: Religious and spiritual issues

It is perhaps one of the great ironies in contemporary professional education, training and practice that religious and spiritual issues are often neglected. After all, much of the impetus that encouraged people into the caring professions not all that long ago came from the religious convictions of individuals who felt that such careers were a legitimate and worthwhile expression of the faith that they held. The origins of the Probation Service can be found in the work that court mission-aries performed. Within the Christian tradition, great store has been laid on care for others, especially those in need, with a strong emphasis upon social justice. Other great religious traditions, including Judaism and Islam, share similar values in this respect.

The contrast with the contemporary situation could hardly be more marked. The reasons for this are many, but perhaps a few points deserve mention:

- There has been a steady decline in formal religious observance and practice during the past few decades.
- Secularization, and now postmodernist thought, have raised large question marks over belief systems and their validity.
- Some religious people seem keen to 'convert' at all costs and on all occasions, and this arouses suspicions in human services agencies for fear that vulner-able people may be inappropriately proselytized.
- The upsurge of religious interest from the late 1990s onwards seems to be among the more fundamentalist groups who often take a very hard line on such issues as abortion and homosexuality and are seen therefore to be at odds with caring values. Religion can be an oppressive as well as a creative experience.
- Some people find the subject faintly embarrassing and uncomfortable and prefer to ignore it altogether. People workers who belong to faith commu-nities sense the ambivalence, even hostility towards religious issues lying just below the surface in many settings and choose to keep quiet about it.

Alongside all of this, however, must go an acknowledgement that, for many members of our multicultural and multifaith society, religious and spiritual issues are important. Many members of minority ethnic groups have a strong religious faith that is expressed through membership of their community (Muslims and Jews, for example). The issue of religious and spiritual needs is recognized in, for example, the Children Act 1989 and has particular import-ance in fostering and adoption practice. When working with people who are dying or bereaved, the large questions about life and death and the meanings we give to them frequently raise spiritual and religious questions that human services professionals need to be able to discuss, whatever their own particular stance on this issue may be.

> **Reflective moment**
>
> How do your own views and feelings about religion and spirituality affect your values and your approach to your work and to your life more broadly?

Consider the following scenarios:

- A devout Muslim wishes to pray at the prescribed times in the workplace and to have as holidays some of the Muslim holy days.
- A resident in a care home wishes to receive holy communion regularly, but no space is put aside or made available for such religious purposes.
- Following a divorce, the mother insists on the young children being with her every Sunday so that they can go to church with her, rather than going out for the day with their father.
- A social worker in a hospital setting is asked for advice by the medical team about a patient who is refusing a blood transfusion on religious grounds.
- A couple whose child has been killed tragically in a road accident want to talk to a nurse about how they can reconcile this with their religious faith.
- A social worker is told by the family they are working with that one of the daughters is about to undergo a clitoridectomy (female circumcision).

There are religious aspects to each of these scenarios, and it would be useful for you to spend some time reflecting on what you perceive these to be and making some notes.

Reflective practice

Unfortunately, much practice in the people professions is driven by habit, unthinking response and copying others. As Thompson and Thompson (2023) point out, this has the effect of bypassing our critical faculties and also, of course, our values. Reflective practice is, by contrast, thoughtful, intelligent practice rooted in professional knowledge, skills and values (Thompson, 2023).

This approach owes a lot to the seminal contribution of Schön (1983, 1987), but it has been widely adopted and discussed in a wide range of literature for the helping professions. It is a significant part of good practice because it encourages critical analysis, effective use of our professional knowledge and skills, but also – importantly – our values. The more we operate on automatic pilot, the more vulnerable we are to acting in ways that are not consistent with our values.

The focus is clearly on each worker and the responsibility we all bear to ensure that we are reviewing our practice, not just from the perspective of updating our knowledge, but for ensuring that our value base is strong and relevant and is informing and underpinning what we do.

Reflective practice presents a challenge to us to retain our freshness in work settings that are often emotionally draining, and to take positive steps to avoid burnout. It is safe to assume that, if we simply let things run their course in whatever setting we are conducting our professional practice as people workers, we will sooner or later lose our creativity and slip into a mechanistic, routinized, process-driven style of working that loses its essential humanity. It is only when we take care of ourselves, personally and professionally, that we safeguard ourselves against this and maintain the sharp edge of our values-based practice.

There is an emphasis in reflective practice on the importance of taking responsibility for our learning and continuing professional development. Many workers, of course, are in agencies where this is a structured aspect of the expectations that managers have and where supervision helps people plan this process. Even so, there can be no substitute for personal responsibility – the more self-directed our learning is, the more effective that learning is likely to be, as it will be more closely linked to our own learning needs, circumstances and preferences.

If we are committed to a journey of ongoing professional development, we will never fall into the trap of feeling that we have got it 'sussed' completely. We will always be open to new understanding and new awareness of the implications of what it means to offer a values-based practice. Self-directed learning and reflective practice are important parts of this.

Reflexive practice

Another important element of reflective practice is reflexivity – that is, the ability – and willingness – to look at ourselves, our assumptions and common behaviours and, of course, our values. Reflexive practice is therefore something worth exploring in a little more detail. We start by revisiting self-location.

We have previously mentioned how, in Ancient Greece, travellers often made their way to the Oracle at Delphi for some wise insight into the future and were confronted at the entrance with the injunction: know thyself. Although it is unlikely that students these days will have to take part in 1960s-style encounter groups, it is still important that we are aware of ourselves, our attitudes and values, and the ways in which they can affect other people. The phrase often used for describing this process is 'locating yourself', the importance of which we have already emphasized.

Our own 'self-location' is also our own agenda, as far as professional people work is concerned, and that is part of our ongoing responsibility to see 'where the shoe pinches' as far as our professional approach to people is concerned. We need to know where we are likely to encounter resistance and suspicion, and therefore where we need to work doubly hard to establish a trusting relationship in our professional practice.

Conclusion

We earlier discussed in some detail the theory base for values and explored various topics that deal with the hugely important themes of discrimination and the oppression it gives rise to. We argued that best practice could not be seen in isolation from these major aspects of contemporary society; rather, they needed to take them seriously. Best practice in fact is synonymous with anti-discriminatory practice, and without this wider societal context, individual work with people is likely to be of limited significance.

Developing values-based practice is not an easy or simple task. It involves reflexively questioning our own assumptions – assumptions that may have been reinforced in us over a period of decades. It also involves challenging others – individuals and organizations – so that we can genuinely say that our work neither discriminates unfairly nor condones unfair discrimination on the part of others. Developing values-based practice in terms of discrimination and oppression is a long and difficult undertaking. It is a matter of values – valuing everybody, regardless of who they are or what social group or category of people they are part of – and so it is something we must wrestle with constantly. It is a process that will continue throughout your career if you are serious about values-based practice.

Because this is a difficult and demanding process, you may well feel tempted at times to pass it by and just 'get on with the job'. We very much hope that you will be able to resist this temptation. The subtle operation of mechanisms of discrimination and oppression have been ignored and misunderstood for long enough. Now that we are becoming increasingly aware of the workings of discrimination and the destructive impact on significant numbers of people, it would be a great pity to slow down the progress we are making. So, if you are tempted to give up playing your part, we would urge you to remember three things:

1. Good practice must be anti-discriminatory practice.
2. Discrimination works in subtle and insidious ways. If we are not sensitive to this, we are likely to condone or reinforce oppression without realizing it. In short, if we are not part of the solution, we must be part of the problem.
3. You are not alone. Anti-discriminatory practice and values are necessary for all of us. Talk to your colleagues about the issues and share the responsibility together. For values-based practice to become a reality, and remain so, a collective effort is needed.

We very much hope that you will be able to play your part in promoting anti-discriminatory values. It will be a difficult process, perhaps painful at times, but we owe it to the people we work with to make it a success.

Exercise 4

It was stated earlier that most discrimination is unintentional, in the sense that, for every deliberate act, there will be many unintentional ones (based on stereotypes, for example). How can you ensure, as far as possible, that you are not unwittingly perpetuating discrimination? How might you tactfully and constructively challenge others who are doing so?

Working in partnership

Introduction

The concept of partnership working, in whatever field of people work we may happen to be practising, takes us to the heart of the contemporary value base of such work. But the calls for this have not always been heeded in everyday practice. Sad to say, this plea for professional accountability and a commitment to partnership working is not new; the need for effective partnership working has been powerfully articulated, certainly within children and family work, for several decades. Tragedy upon tragedy has highlighted the need for professionals to communicate effectively. A recurring theme of official reports over decades has been the failure of professionals to work together that has cost the lives of vulnerable children and young people (Wilkinson *et al.*, 2019).

Not that this is restricted to children and young people: in the mental health field there has been widespread concern at the lack of joined-up services for vulnerable adults, and the issues of elder abuse have also raised similar concerns in terms of the lack of effective multidisciplinary working.

It is important to clarify the value base implicit in partnership working. Social workers, education staff, mental health professionals and various representatives of the medical profession and/or professions allied to medicine: upon these and other colleagues there rests an expectation that they regard each other in a far more holistic way than in the past. Each discipline needs to understand its role and purpose, but there needs also to be a wider appreciation that *only together* can a full picture be obtained, and *only together* can the full range of effective services

DOI: 10.4324/9781003689614-6

be provided. Crucially, as the reports have shown so often, *only when* there is effective professional partnership working can major tragedies be averted.

But this is now seen only to be part of the wider picture. No longer should the professionals be seen as the experts who know all the answers, and whose role, separately and together, is simply to gather enough information in order to inform their expert decision making. Increasingly we are coming to realize that the professionals are not the only ones with expertise: the very people we serve also have much to contribute. The term 'co-production' is now increasingly being used to refer to the joint working between helper and helped and it captures nicely the idea of partnership as not just an activity, but also an important value. This is authentic partnership working, all concerned bringing their respective expertise to pool resources and develop a holistic picture of the situation.

This represents for some a huge change in thinking and approach to their work. It is one thing to value another professional, and this takes some doing for some workers. But then, to make the quantum leap into *really* valuing the people we serve and into stating that *they* so often are the real experts in their lives is radically to reshape the value base of assessment and intervention.

The frequently cited classic model that supports this approach is the 'exchange model' (Smale *et al.,* 1993). This model unashamedly assumes that people have expertise in their own lives, and that the role of the worker is to work closely with the people we serve to come up with a range of responses that can most effectively address the issues being raised, within the constraints of resources that are so often in short supply. The central issue here is that the role of clients is seen to be far more than a mere passive recipient of services. Instead, they play a key role in carving out the way forward. And this clearly has major implications for practice and, most importantly of all, for the value base of the work being undertaken.

Key point

If we are to take the people we serve seriously and to place them centre stage, then this will test out our value base probably more than anything else. Such an approach requires us *really to value* clients *as people*, rather than as some second-class citizens who need to be grateful for the ways in which we render them a service. More than that, it lays upon us an obligation to have a degree of humility that we do not always (perhaps ever?) know best.

We recognize that the use of the word 'humility' may jar a little for some people, either because they do not 'buy into' the religious connotations it may hold or because it smacks of a servile attitude that is wholly inappropriate for any aspect of people work. In its true sense, however, the word humility implies a willingness to listen to someone else, to put them centre stage, and to acknowledge that only through a genuine commitment to partnership working with the people who use our services will a truly satisfactory outcome be achieved.

Some examples from practice

Some examples will illustrate the point we are making here. Again, these are real-life examples, but duly anonymized. As you read them, think about what values issues they raise:

1. Hifsa worked as an adviser in a Citizens Advice Bureau and began to work with Paulette who arrived with a plastic bag full of unpaid debts and a threat of eviction. Paulette's initial reaction was to try to dump everything onto Hifsa to sort out, as the 'expert' in these matters. Hifsa was sensitive enough, however, to realize that Paulette was the real expert in terms of knowing what she and her family needed. Slowly she gained her confidence and worked together with her to prioritize the debts and to decide a plan of action in which each of them had a role to play. Initially, Hifsa needed to act swiftly in her role as adviser to deal with the threat of eviction, but Paulette soon began to realize that the more she was involved in trying to sort matters out, the better were her long-term chances of turning the corner and building a new life.

2. Anton worked as a detached youth worker in a large city centre. He spent a lot of time 'creatively loitering' in the areas where 'disaffected young people' (as they are sometimes called by professionals) congregated most evenings. One evening he was confronted by Shane, an irate teenager who berated him for the ills of society and for not finding him a decent job and somewhere to sleep. Tempted though Anton was to slip away and avoid further confrontation he decided against it and heard him out. He then suggested that they went for a walk to an all-night café where, over a period of several hours, the story of neglect and abuse came out, detail by painful detail. The story had never been told before, and at the end Anton praised him for the trust Shane had shown by telling him the story. Together they then began to work out how to turn Shane's life around, both in terms of individual plans and also by agreeing that it was important to report the abuse to the relevant authorities, so that the perpetrator could be brought to account. It was this possibility, and Anton's willingness to facilitate it, that convinced Shane that his future could be brighter and more hopeful.

3. Faith worked in a women's refuge and constantly faced a barrage of requests from the women to do things for them. Fortunately, she quickly recognized that people can easily become institutionalized, especially after traumatic experiences that have left them with low self-esteem and no self-confidence. She also recognized that they could also experience 'learned helplessness' that would serve no useful purpose when they returned to live in the community. She therefore instituted a system whereby, instead of having free access

to her in the office at any time, each resident was allocated at least one session per week that was devoted to exploring their strengths and the ways in which they could begin, after their painful experiences of violence and disempowerment, to retake responsibility for their lives and the decisions that felt right for them.

4.   Washington was a social worker with particular responsibility for working with people with a variety of impairments. His visits to Mabel became a source of worry for him because Mabel had lost most of her sight and her two daughters regularly requested that he 'do something about it and get her into a home where she would be cared for properly and no longer be a risk to herself and others'. Initially, he felt very pressurized by the daughters and went so far as to locate some sheltered accommodation that seemed to be suitable for Mabel. When, on his next visit he broached this with Mabel, he was stunned by the fierceness of her opposition to his plans. Instead of becoming authoritarian or defensive, he spent time listening to Mabel and then made arrangements for a detailed assessment of her needs that resulted in some adaptations being made and some help with household tasks. Mabel was delighted that she could stay in the home she knew and loved and was not going to be pushed out 'into a place full of strangers'.

5.   Annabel worked in a child protection team and dreaded the meeting with the Forsters that numerous complaints had been made about in relation to the welfare of their two children. It seemed at face value that the children would need to be received into care for their safety and protection. With a colleague she arranged to visit the family and was met with initial hostility. Keeping calm, she explained her role and the responsibility that she shared with the family in keeping the children safe. She explained that, as a last resort, the children might well be placed in care, but that she would do whatever she could to work with the family to help improve things at home. She further explained that she would be doing her job really well if she were able to work creatively with the parents to improve their parenting and the life chances of their children.

6.   Patrick worked as a probation officer and was becoming exasperated at the way in which Kevin was refusing to cooperate with the conditions of his Probation Order. In the end, he had no alternative but to return him to court. In preparing the report he talked again at length with Kevin and explained to him that, although the decisions about returning him to court were his to make as the probation officer, he could only really work with him if he recognized that partnership working was a two-way contract. At this point, Kevin became very hostile and asked how was he expected to deal with all the pressures facing him with two sickly babies at home and a partner who was not coping at all well since the birth of the twins six weeks ago. Patrick was stunned – he simply had not bothered to try to find out how things were at home, so keen was he to ensure that Kevin worked his way through the anger management and offending behaviour programme. He revised his report,

explaining to Kevin that he would seek the court's permission to work with him in a different and more effective way.

Each of these anonymized true examples illustrates not just the issues about what these people workers actually did or did not do; they also illustrate the values issues that permeate each of the scenarios from both the worker's perspective and those who use our services.

TIP! These scenarios highlight how partnership can go awry, but, with appropriate skill and commitment, effective partnership working can be achieved and produce positive results. There is no need to be defeatist about the possibilities.

Working positively with tensions and conflicts

The case examples above all have considerable tensions, conflicts even, inherent in them, for both the worker and the person who uses our services. This raises the important question of how people workers view conflict, and what strategies they employ for handling such situations. We might even say that there is an issue about how people workers *value* conflict.

There are, of course, the two classic responses of fight and flight. Leaving aside for a moment situations in the community where the worker may be at some personal risk, where flight will be the most appropriate response, it is rarely best practice to implement either of these extremes. For some, however, the principle at stake is one of their *authority* and the value base that underpins it. Therefore, it is crucial to them that, in any conflict with a client, they come out on top and assert their authority because, after all, 'as the professional expert, they know best'.

By contrast, others will flinch and do everything in their power to avoid confrontation and the pressure that accompanies it. So, they will put off the difficult home visit where children might be at risk. They will mollify the person on probation and not take them back to court when they do not fulfil the conditions of their order. They will take on lots of tasks *on behalf of* the client, rather than tackle the sometimes complex and challenging task of empowering them. Similarly, this can apply to managers too when they are aware of unacceptable practices but fail to address them. Conflict is to be avoided – not least because the worker or manager wants, even needs, to be liked, and that is a central plank in their own value base as a professional.

Best practice involves a willingness to work positively with tensions created by conflicts of interest or differing intentions and plans. For this to happen, the worker needs to have explored the value base of conflict and their attitude towards it. There will, of course, be times where an immediate resolution is impossible, where a worker needs to exercise legal powers to remove someone for their safety or that of others. Then there is no 'beating about the bush' – it has to happen. But even so, how this is explained to people, and importantly, how this is followed up in terms of working and seeking to build trust, is of fundamental importance. It reflects the issue raised earlier in the discussion about valuing the people we serve and seeing that they are important in themselves. It may be that they have temporarily lost sight of their capacity to care for others, perhaps through misuse of drugs or alcohol, but this does not mean that the worker should give up on the task of working with them to help them restore these capabilities.

TIP! Many people have a fear of conflict and will therefore tend to avoid it wherever possible, possibly to the extent of burying their head in the sands. A much wiser approach is to face up to it and develop the skills for addressing conflict constructively.

Wider community networks

The value base of partnership, as we have seen, has been expanded. From a realization that professionals need to work together where possible as a team, there has grown a deeper understanding that those who use our services not only belong to the team as *recipients of a service*; they also should be seen as the leading players. The National Health Service has a vision of a patient-led health service, and this captures and expresses the value base of people work very clearly.

However, there is a still wider dimension to this debate that brings a further challenge to the understanding we have about our value base. The contribution that community networks can play in the 'health of the nation' in all aspects of that term cannot be underestimated. For a while, governments in this country and in America were lauding the voluntary sector and encouraging it to maximize its contribution to community services. This concept was further enhanced with the communitarian initiatives espoused by Etzioni (1995) in particular, where community initiatives were often regarded as the major players in the team. Further initiatives in community capacity building have strengthened this development and have presented people workers with another challenge to their value base. How are we to regard such developments?

Once again, we can see the 'flight and fight' responses – or perhaps more accurately a 'jump or dump' mentality. Some will jump in the opposite direction and refuse to have anything to do with such community-based resources. They are regarded with suspicion or presented with so many bureaucratic hoops to jump through if they wish to have funding for projects that they give up after the first deluge of paperwork. They thereby confirm the opinion of the professional people workers that they are 'ineffective amateurs dabbling in things they don't understand'. It is therefore best to leave it to the experts.

By contrast, other workers will see these organizations as the cavalry arriving to relieve the besieged fortress of social care. They gladly dump a wide range of tasks and responsibilities upon them and breathe a sigh of relief that their work-load can be reduced.

Neither approach, of course, captures what a true commitment to partner-ship working should be like. The hope is that people workers will see that a true commitment to the value base of partnership will involve treating voluntary and private organizations as valued members of the team who have an important role to play. But for this to be achieved, it will require the people workers to look care-fully at their value base to see whether they really do value such groups as equal and important partners, or as some second-class group who can perhaps offer some limited first aid, but precious little else.

Key point

It is essential for effective partnership working to be able to see situations from the point of view of the other people involved, rather than just try to impose our perspective on them.

An example from practice: Faith communities

One area where this issue can be acute is the involvement of faith communities in the wider sphere of health and social care. It is perhaps one of the 'blind spots' in health and social care provision that professional workers fail to appreciate the volume and quality of care that faith communities provide up and down the country. And often this is not just for those who belong to them as the members or adherents; often faith community projects will be for the wider benefit of the community at large, with no expectations of religious allegiance or commitment. A wide range of provision exists, from crèche and nursery/playgroup facilities; youth clubs and young people's activities; parenting support; sports facilities; lunch clubs and social clubs for elders; to hospital visiting schemes. The list is a long one, but it is not often that professional people workers acknowledge the richness of the provision or seek to work in active partnerships (for a fur-ther discussion on the role of faith communities in this context, see for example Smith, 2001).

For some, this is in itself a values issue, in that they are suspicious of the intentions of faith communities, and suspect that their ulterior motives will involve proselytizing, and perhaps taking advantage of vulnerable members of the community. These are important issues to consider and should be on the agenda in an open and honest way when collaborative partnerships are being explored. But, to rule out any partnership working without exploring these issues in depth is to draw the line in such a way as to exclude *on principle* such partnership possibilities. And that is as much an expression of the value base of the worker as it is of the organization concerned.

TIP! If you are not already aware of what support services provided by faith communities are available in your area, there is much to be gained from making the effort to find out.

Conclusion

This chapter has explored partnership working as a major theme in the value base of professional people work. It has traced the development of interprofessional working from the failure of different professional groups actively to collaborate in protecting and empowering vulnerable members of society. It has noted that the value base of partnership has been increasingly widened not only to include the people who use our services as key players, but also the wider community.

Throughout the discussion the focus has been upon values, not policies or procedures or detailed legislation, although all of these flow from a value base, and have implications for how a value base informs practice. The argument throughout has been to show that it will be the value base that has the most powerful impact upon practice, whether or not that has been clearly understood or articulated. It is the basic premise of this manual that unless the value base we have as people workers is understood, examined and explored, then we will not be able to deliver that gold standard of best practice to which we should be committed. This chapter has argued that, only when the value base of partnership is fully appreciated – when professionals; service users and carers, and community groups are seen as equally important members of the team – will best practice stand a chance of becoming a reality.

The underlying challenge to regard others as equal partners carries with it a further challenge: that of recognizing, respecting and celebrating diversity, as we discussed earlier.

Exercise 5

What do you see as the main obstacles to effective partnership working? What steps can be taken to avoid, remove or reduce them or minimize their impact?

Rights and choice

Introduction

Our focus in this chapter is on another important aspect of values-based practice, namely the significance of rights and choice. If people are being denied their rights or are not being given choices, then we can hardly say that we are working in a values-based way, in the sense that we are using that term here. We begin, then, by considering the importance of rights and choice as values issues.

Why are rights and choice important?

Rights and choice are both important aspects of human dignity and are therefore an essential part of the value base of social care. People in need of social care are, first and foremost, citizens and, as such, have basic rights. In this chapter, we shall look in more detail at what these rights are and how these can be safeguarded. Also, we need to be clear about the circumstances in which an individual's rights can be overruled, either for the person's own good or for the protection of others. Choice is also an important part of citizenship, an essential part of living a satisfying and fulfilling life. Choice is about having some degree of control over one's life. The absence of choice is therefore both oppressive and, as we shall see, a significant source of stress and distress.

What are rights?

The *Webster's Third New International Dictionary* defines a right as: 'something to which one has a just claim ... the power or privilege to which one is justly

DOI: 10.4324/9781003689614-7

entitled', a definition that seems to hinge on two key concepts: justice, or fairness, and entitlement. Fairness is, of course, a central value in the human services and reflects the importance of an approach based on equality and social justice.

Entitlement implies that a right is not a matter of discretion, it is not something that can be withheld without good reason. Clearly, then, rights are an important part of the value base of working with people in need of support and/or protection. Understanding people's rights, and working sensitively and effectively with them, is therefore a fundamental aspect of good practice. Perhaps the best way to understand rights is to look at a range of examples and consider, briefly at least, some of the implications for practice. This is precisely what we shall do now.

Clients have a right to ...

Equality of treatment

As we have made clear, equality and the freedom from discrimination it encapsulates is a primary value in people work. It is, of course, also a fundamental right and one we would do well not to ignore. It is clearly a matter of good practice to ensure that people are not unfairly treated on the basis of gender, race, ethnic group, age, disability, sexual identity or any other such factors. It is therefore vitally important that we are sensitive to the potential for discrimination and unfair treatment, as we have already emphasized.

Privacy

In group care settings there is sometimes a problem over privacy. There can be difficulties in trying to give people the space to be on their own when they feel the need to. However, we should be careful to ensure that we do not become defeatist about this and assume that privacy is not possible. It is important that a person's wish for privacy is respected as the absence of privacy can lead to considerable tension, distress and even depression. A common mistake as far as privacy is concerned is to assume that people who enjoy the company of others do not want or need privacy. The important point here is that people should be given the choice – an issue to which we shall return below. Privacy is particularly important with regard to personal matters, such as bathing, toileting and so on. This can be a difficult issue for people whose personal care needs are quite extensive and who may need direct assistance in such matters. In such cases, the need for staff to handle the situation with great sensitivity and dignity is paramount.

Information and consultation

Helping is not something that we do *to* people, but rather *with* them. It is therefore important that clients are fully involved in planning, both on a day-to-day basis and in the longer term. For this to be effective it is necessary for full consultation to take place at every stage and for no information to be withheld. Information and consultation are essential parts of partnership and empowerment – key aspects of the process of helping people gain as much control as possible over their lives and circumstances. It is therefore important that our practice contributes positively to this process by ensuring appropriate consultation and information, as a failure to do so can be seen as a significant denial of a basic right.

Confidentiality
Just as there is a right to receive information, so too is there a right for information about, or from, clients to be treated in confidence, subject to the constraints already discussed in Chapter 3.

Individuality and identity
Each of us has a right to be treated as a unique individual and a person in their own right. The implications of this form the subject matter of the next chapter, and so we shall not comment further at this stage.

Respect and self-respect
Respect is a quality that is rather intangible, but none the less important and worthy of attention. Having respect for people involves:

- being prepared to listen;
- not trying to impose your own view;
- going at their pace;
- taking account of their feelings and needs;
- not being condescending or overbearing; and
- not seeing yourself as being in any way superior.

Good practice must therefore not only recognize these points but also ensure that they are adhered to – that is, based in reality rather than just paid lip service. Self-respect is an extension of this and is closely related to self-esteem, the value we place upon ourselves. Simply put, self-respect and therefore self-esteem will be seriously hampered by an absence of respect on the part of others.

Honesty and openness
This follows on from the previous point. We can hardly claim to be dealing with people in a respectful way if we are less than honest or if we keep secrets. For people to feel secure and settled there must be an atmosphere of mutual trust. Such an atmosphere is, of course, not possible, unless complete honesty is established as the norm. Even the slightest example of dishonesty can destroy months or even years of building up trust and mutual respect.

Their own culture

Cultural customs, practices, expectations and beliefs play a major part in our lives. For these to be overridden, ignored, marginalized, discredited or ridiculed is clearly a form of oppression and therefore, by definition, bad practice. Good practice therefore needs to be 'ethnically sensitive' or 'culturally competent', aware of, and responsive to, different cultural values and needs. This is an important part of anti-discriminatory practice. However, we should note that this is not simply a matter of differences between black and white. Within both black and white communities there is a considerable diversity of cultures in terms of:

■ language;
■ religion; and
■ national or regional identity.

Such differences can manifest themselves in a variety of ways (for example, diet) and can have major implications for professional practice. If our attempts to provide care are not to prove oppressive, we must ensure that we take full account of the cultural background of the people we work with.

> **Key point**
>
> It is essential that we do not allow cultural **differences** to be seen as cultural **deficits**. The tendency to see other cultures as inferior or as a threat is a common feature of racism.

Protection from abuse

Abuse is, by definition, something to be avoided, something from which we all need to be protected as far as possible. In general, the more vulnerable a person is, the greater the risk of abuse. As people in need of support are so often vulnerable in some way, they tend to be more prone to abuse than others (consider, for example, both child abuse and the abuse of older people – 'elder abuse'). In order to protect people from abuse, we need to:

■ be sensitive to the possibility of abuse and recognize the danger signs;
■ be aware of policies and procedures relating to abuse and the responsibilities these place on us;
■ share any concerns we may have with our line manager or senior colleague; and
■ ensure that our own actions and attitudes are in no way abusive.

The right to protection from abuse is an extremely important right for, without this right, so many other rights lose all meaning.

Representation and complaints

People have a right to make complaints where necessary and to be represented. This is important for two reasons:

1. Knowing that access to a helpful complaints procedure is available gives them a sense of security, a safety net that can reassure them that they will be listened to if there is anything they are unhappy about.
2. Similarly, from the staff's point of view, the complaints procedure can act as a spur to good practice by:

   - identifying possible areas of bad practice and thus providing learning opportunities;
   - clearing up possible misunderstandings or tension: between staff and service users;
   - emphasizing the need for high-quality care.

It is important, therefore, that the complaints procedure is not seen in a negative light as a threat or a problem. It has a very positive and constructive role to play in ensuring that the care provided is of the highest quality possible within the resources available.

Reflective moment

Does your employing organization have a Representation and Complaints procedure? If so, what are your obligations under this procedure? (What do you need to know and what do you need to do?). If there is no official procedure, what do your employers expect of you in this respect? Are you clear what your role is and how you should proceed if a complaint needs to be made?

Review of care

Once care arrangements are established, the planning task is, of course, not complete. These arrangements need to be reviewed to take account of changing circumstances or new information gained. Satisfactory care arrangements can become very unsatisfactory if the situation is not reviewed on a regular basis.

Good practice

In a sense, this is the sum of all the other rights. Without good practice clients can be harmed, rather than helped, oppressed rather than empowered. Having a need for care means being dependent, to a certain extent, on staff. This makes people very vulnerable to the negative effects of practice.

Rights are, of course, closely linked with duties. As we have seen, clients have a number of important rights, and so this means that staff have certain duties. Perhaps the most important of these duties, and certainly the central one, is the duty to avoid bad practice wherever possible, the duty to ensure that the standards of care provided are the best possible within the resources available.

The significance of choice

The notion of choice implies two sets of issues, both of which have a major bearing on values-based practice:

1. *Options*: There needs to be a range of options available for choice to have any real meaning. Do the people you work with have real choices? Do you play a part in increasing these options and do you make sure people know what options are available?
2. *The opportunity to choose*: Clearly, it is no good having options available if people are not given the opportunity to choose, if decisions are made for them or, if no consultation takes place. It is not enough to have options available in theory – there must be genuine choice in practice.

It must be remembered that choice is not a luxury but, rather, an essential element of good-quality care. We cannot expect people to have dignity and self-respect and to feel happy and settled unless they have as much control over their lives as possible – that is, that they are empowered.

When should rights and choice be overridden?

This is a difficult but, none the less, important question, and one that we have already encountered in relation to confidentiality. The key word here is risk and relates to the sort of situation in which exercising a particular right or choice may place someone in danger. This applies in two ways:

1. *Danger to others*: The risk factors are likely to vary across the different client groups but the common theme is that certain restrictions on a person's rights or choice may be necessary in order to safeguard others (for example, a prohibition on smoking in certain areas).
2. *Danger to oneself*: This is less clear-cut and places us in something of a moral dilemma. Certain actions can place people at risk of injury or even death but do we have the right to protect people from their own actions even if this goes against their wishes? In general terms, the answer is 'no', although we do have a duty to dissuade people from harmful actions.

It is clearly the second aspect, danger to oneself, that is more complex and more difficult to deal with. A helpful concept in trying to wrestle with these issues is that of responsibility. It is our responsibility to try to discourage or dissuade people from taking steps that can, or will, lead to self-harm. However, we are not responsible for the consequences if they decide to go ahead regardless of our discouragement or disapproval, except in the case of any of the following three sets of circumstances applying:

1. *The self-harm would also be a danger to others*: Sometimes we can concentrate so much on the element of self-harm that we lose track of the possibility of harm to others.
2. *The person concerned is a child*: Here it is necessary to act *in loco parentis* and to protect the child from harm.
3. *The person concerned is mentally disordered or has severe learning difficulties*: In such situations, mental health legislation will apply and you will need to get specialist help.

Any situation that involves denying someone their rights or choice is a very serious one that should not be taken lightly. It is advisable that, wherever you encounter such a situation – actually or potentially – you seek the advice of your line manager or a senior colleague.

Conclusion
In developing values-based practice, rights and choice are bound to play a significant part. As we have seen, it is both a complex and vitally important area, a key aspect of good practice that places a range of demands on people professionals. Earlier, under the heading of 'Clients have a right to ... Good practice', the point was made that a set of rights implies a set of duties. This chapter of the manual has, we hope, helped you to form a picture of what those duties are and how you might tackle them. We hope it has also shown you how important these matters are and has encouraged you to learn more about them and develop your knowledge and skills further.

Exercise 6
In what ways might the denial of rights and choice lead to problems such as conflict, aggression and violence, mental health problems and problematic drug use? What connections can you draw?

Individuality and identity

Introduction

To be denied our individuality and identity is to be disempowered. Consequently, we need to make sure that, in developing values-based practice, we are tuned in to people's individuality and identity. There is a tendency to take these matters for granted and therefore be unaware of the problems that can arise for those people who find themselves in situations where their sense of who they are is being undermined or totally disregarded.

Why are individuality and identity important?

As with rights and choice, individuality and identity are important aspects of human dignity. If people feel they are not being treated as individuals, but simply as part of a wider group, it is likely that they will feel that their needs are not being recognized and that they are not being valued as a person in their own right. Such an experience can be a profoundly alienating and dehumanizing one and, therefore, very oppressive. People in need of social care may well have much in common, but we should not allow this to distract us from the fact that each one is a unique individual with a specific identity.

What are individuality and identity?

In some ways, all people are the same. For example, we all need to eat, drink, breathe and so on. In some ways, some people are the same and some are different. For example, in terms of age, gender, culture and other social group

DOI: 10.4324/9781003689614-8

membership, we will have much in common with certain groups of people but will be very different from others. In some ways, all people are unique, with their own personal beliefs, feelings and needs. It is at this third level that individuality and identity are very much to the fore. Identity is, of course, a shorthand term for who we are, the sense of self that we have and is therefore in part a spiritual matter in terms of our sense of who we are and how we fit into the wider world.

Our sense of self can be divided into (at least) two main elements – self-image and self-esteem:

■ Self-image describes the view we have of ourselves, the image on which we base our thoughts, feelings and actions. For example, it is recognized that people suffering from anorexia nervosa tend to have an image of themselves as fat, even though they are, in reality, quite thin.
■ Self-esteem refers to the value we place on ourselves, how highly we think of ourselves. High self-esteem is associated with confidence and a positive attitude, whilst low self-esteem is associated with feelings of worthlessness, low motivation and, in extreme cases, depression.

Both these concepts, self-image and self-esteem, are important in providing high-quality practice. We therefore need to make sure that we contribute, as far as possible, to a positive self-image and high self-esteem.

Personal beliefs
A person's beliefs and values are an important part of their sense of identity and are a key part of:

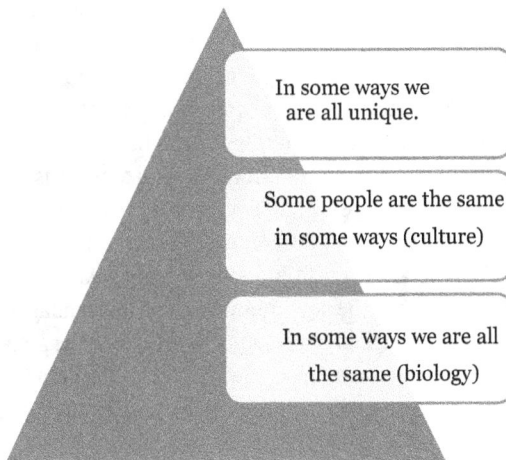

In some ways we
are all unique.

Some people are the same
in some ways (culture)

In some ways we are all
the same (biology)

Figure 7.1 Aspects of identity

- *The past* – previous life experiences and socialization;
- *The present* – our beliefs have a significant influence on our actions and attitudes;
- *The future* – our wishes, aspirations and plans.

Key point

A key issue when it comes to beliefs is hope. How much hope a person has will depend on their beliefs, and their beliefs will depend, to a certain extent at least, on the degree of hope they have – it is a two-way relationship.

What we have to bear in mind, therefore, is that personal beliefs are very significant for the individual. Consequently, to dismiss, disregard or invalidate a person's beliefs is to dismiss, disregard or invalidate the person. Where such beliefs are a reflection of a person's religion or culture, then that religion or culture can be under attack too. It is to be hoped that we would not act in such a way intentionally, although such problems do arise at certain times. However, what is much more likely to happen than a deliberate attack on someone's beliefs or culture is to cause offence unintentionally. The underlying problem is therefore more likely to be one of insensitivity or lack of awareness than one of malice. Consequently, an important aspect of good practice in terms of individualism and identity is to develop a sensitivity to matters of culture, religion and language – to develop what was called earlier ethnically sensitive practice.

It is also important to recognize that there can be a conflict between your own beliefs and those of the people you work with. Sometimes, this is open, and it is easy to see the differences. However, at other times, the differences can be more hidden and implicit – more difficult to spot but, none the less, powerful in their influence and their potential for conflict. An example of the latter would be differences based on class background. Sometimes, people from different backgrounds feel uncomfortable with each other, but cannot quite put their finger on what the problem is. When such situations arise, it is important to recognize what is happening, so that tensions between you do not increase and lead to a problematic situation. It is a good idea to try to work out just what the differences are between you, so that you can try to find common ground and establish a good working relationship. In order to do this, you may need to talk over the situation with your line manager or someone else you trust, someone who can take a more objective view of the situation.

Our beliefs and values are, in a sense, the spectacles through which we view the world. As such, they have a significant impact on our day-to-day lives in terms of:

- our tastes and preferences;
- what motivates us;

- what we find offensive;
- what makes us feel comfortable or uncomfortable; and
- our hopes and fears.

They are therefore very much *values* issues. For this reason, it is essential, from the point of view of good practice, to understand what people's beliefs and values are and, as far as possible, to respect them.

Knowing and assuming

A lot of the time we get these two mixed up – we often act as if we know something when, in fact, we are making an assumption. Of course, it would be impossible to check everything out and make sure of our facts. It is inevitable that we will have to rely on assumptions to a certain extent. However, what tends to be very problematic is when we do not appreciate the difference between knowing and assuming. This is particularly the case in terms of stereotypes.

Stereotypes are fixed and rigid views of certain people or groups of people that we are unlikely to change, even in the face of strong evidence to the contrary. A stereotype is therefore a form of prejudice – a pre-judgement or false generalization that distorts our perception of the person or the group of people:

> The concept of stereotyping is a particularly important one in relation to discrimination and oppression. Dominance, inequality and injustice are often maintained by reference to stereotypes – for example, of disabled people, gay men, lesbians or bisexuals. Stereotypes are therefore powerful tools of ideology and are thus significant obstacles to the development of anti-discriminatory practice.
>
> (Thompson, 2021, p. 46)

What this shows is that there is a danger of being too rigid or dogmatic in our beliefs. It is important that we are able to be flexible and responsive, rather than allow ourselves to get stuck in the tramlines of stereotypical thinking. It is essential that we get to know the individual, rather than simply make assumptions about them, otherwise there is a danger that we are making a false generalization – an experience that could be profoundly alienating or oppressive for the person concerned. A particularly problematic aspect of this is when clients become stereotyped as a group in their own right – ageist stereotypes of older people, for example.

This can manifest itself in a residential care context in the very harmful process of institutionalization in which individualism and personal identity are swallowed up in the interests of simplifying the situation, so that it is easier for staff to deal with. We need to be very wary of this process, as it is a very destructive one. People become treated just as examples of 'the sort of people we have here', rather than as individuals in their own right. Often, the language used can reflect or reinforce this process of 'de-individualization'. For example, terms like 'the elderly' or 'the handicapped' are very impersonal and have derogatory overtones. Terms like 'older people' or 'people with a disability' are far less problematic and are therefore very much to be preferred.

Guidelines for good practice

Getting to grips with the complex issues of individualism and identity can be quite tricky and demanding. To help you with this task, the remainder of this chapter is devoted to a number of guidelines for good practice – practical pointers to help you develop your skills and confidence in this area. It is to be hoped that these guidelines will help you, and encourage you, to think further about the issues, rather than simply provide you with a set of DOs and DON'Ts that you follow unthinkingly.

1. Respect people's rights

As we noted in Chapter 6, rights and choice play an important part in values-based practice. We can now further recognize that undermining a person's rights also amounts to undermining their individuality by devaluing the person and thereby attacking their self-esteem.

2. Be sensitive to cultural issues

As we have seen, a person's cultural background is a central part of their identity or sense of self. We must therefore make sure that we take account of such matters by developing our knowledge, awareness and understanding of different cultural beliefs, values, practices and needs.

3. Adopt an anti-racist approach

Whilst it is clearly important to develop an ethnically sensitive, culturally competent approach, this on its own is not enough. We also have to recognize that some sectors of society devalue certain cultures and see them as inferior. This being the case, many clients will have experienced racism, and the hostility and rejection this entails. This has three sets of implications:

- These issues need to be taken into account in terms of your assessment of people's needs and circumstances;
- You need to make sure your own actions and attitudes do not unwittingly reinforce such racism; and
- You need to challenge and undermine racism whenever you encounter it.

4. Acknowledge the individual as a person

Sometimes, in dealing with a lot of people, and with a lot of tasks to complete, we can slip into bad habits of forgetting to treat people as individuals. When this happens, we limit ourselves to meeting basic needs and lose track of higher goals of quality of life and the need to feel valued as a person in our own right. Being busy explains why this often gets forgotten but, of course, it does not excuse it.

5. Be prepared to listen

If we work on the basis of stereotypes and assumptions, we do not need to listen as we already 'know' the answer. However, if we are to avoid this type of practice, we need to make sure that we are really listening to what people are trying to say to us.

6. Address people appropriately

Our names, and how we are addressed by people, are also important parts of our sense of identity. In order to respect this, we must check how people wish to be addressed. For example, in dealing with adults, beware of assuming that using first names will be interpreted as a sign of friendship. Many people were brought up to see this a sign of a lack of respect and may prefer the use of formal titles (for example, Mr or Mrs) until they get to know you. It does not hurt to ask people how they would prefer to be addressed – but it can hurt to be addressed inappropriately. Similarly, in working with children or adults, beware of using nicknames without first checking that this is acceptable to the person concerned. Do not assume that the nickname is welcomed by the person concerned (or that you have yet earned the right to use that nickname if it is a sign of affection or friendship).

7. Seek guidance where necessary

As we acknowledged before, these are complex matters so do not be afraid to ask your colleagues or your line manager for guidance. It is also helpful to get the views of others on these matters, as they are very personal and you can find it difficult to see them objectively if you do not have the benefit of other people's perspectives. Seeking guidance from others is an important part of learning.

8. Know yourself

This is a bit of a cliché and is certainly easier said than done. However, self-awareness – knowing about your own individuality and identity – is certainly a very helpful and constructive step on the path towards appreciating the importance of these matters for the people you work with. It is to be hoped that our earlier discussions of self-location will have helped you to begin this process and that you will continue with it.

Conclusion

Good practice is clearly based on promoting individuality and identity. Such an approach can be seen to empower people, to give them as much control as possible over their lives, to make a positive contribution to self-esteem and to discourage dependency as far as possible.

In view of this, the challenge to promote individuality and identity is a major one but, none the less, a vital one.

Exercise 7

Consider the following questions and make some notes below (consult with colleagues if you wish):

What stereotype(s) might someone attach to you? Is that what you are really like? Is it helpful to be seen in this way? What problems could a rigid, stereotyped view of you lead to? How would it feel, then, to be treated like this, even though this is not the real you? What are the implications for practice? What should you do to prevent stereotypes from becoming a barrier to good practice?

CHAPTER 8

Valuing diversity

Introduction

'Diversity' has become something of a buzzword over the years, meaning that it is very widely used, but not necessarily widely understood. In this chapter we clarify what is meant by diversity and discuss how it forms an important part of values-based practice.

What is diversity?

Essentially, diversity means variety. It refers to the various differences that mark us out from others. Such differences do not undermine our uniqueness or importance as individuals. On the contrary, they enrich and enhance our individuality, and the contribution that we can make to society. We need to value diversity precisely because of this individual and societal enrichment. But it is this very enrichment that is so powerfully undermined by discrimination.

If we consider the various ways in which people can be discriminated against, such as age, race/ethnicity, culture, disability, gender, religion, sexuality and class, in all these areas, difference can be either celebrated or used as a way of putting people down and regarding them as second-class citizens. What it boils down to is one key question: Do we regard differences across groups and categories of people as sources of variety, interest and enrichment (and therefore as assets to be appreciated) or as a problem to be solved because we are fearful of differences or regard people who are different from us as a threat? Clearly, the idea of valuing or celebrating difference is consistent with the 'assets' answer, while discriminatory actions and attitudes are consistent with the 'problems' answer.

DOI: 10.4324/9781003689614-9

One of the litmus tests of a civilized society is the way in which minority groups are regarded and treated by the majority. This involves the extent to which people who belong to minority groups are marginalized or victimized – in effect, punished for being different from the majority. We would want to argue that a truly mature society is not marked out so much by its tolerance of difference, important though that undoubtedly is, but the extent to which it positively celebrates difference, and cherishes and encourages it as an enrichment.

Events around the world and in the UK in recent years have demonstrated just how perilous and important such a vision for a society has become. In moments of tension or attack, some of the tolerance and acceptance of various groups in society can quickly dissolve. Groups can be targeted and scapegoated, and the cherished principles of a multicultural community (however that is to be defined) are put at risk.

In these situations, the issue of values again comes to the surface in a stark way. We are forced to ask ourselves what sort of society we want to live in and to help shape and direct. We are forced to answer questions about the values we hold, and what we feel about people who are different from ourselves.

These comments help us to locate the theme of diversity against a national, even international background. It is important briefly to acknowledge this context in order to remind ourselves that issues to do with respecting and valuing diversity are not some quirky pastime of the 'politically correct' or 'woke' few, but rather take us to the very heart of the sort of societies we want to see flourishing in the contemporary world.

But here, of course, comes the rub, for part of the wider world perspective reveals that there are indeed some societies (or at least some leaders of societies) whose *raison d'être* profoundly challenges this view about respecting diversity. For them, to accept a celebration of diversity smacks of a liberal *laissez faire* approach that they regard as a slippery slope towards moral anarchy. Such perspectives require a corporate allegiance to a single worldview that brooks no opposition: indeed, diversity is seen as a weakness that has to be challenged. This is a view that is sometimes present in those arguing for a 'purist' Islamic state, for example.

Key point

Values and value systems are part of the fabric of the contemporary world at individual, organizational, national and international levels. While our particular discussion will focus on issues to do with people work in a variety of settings, there will inevitably be occasions when these larger perspectives impinge on our individual practice.

Some examples from practice

Once again, we present some examples of actual practice situations that highlight a range of values issues, in this case, specifically around diversity. As you read them think carefully about what issues they raise and what your views are about these issues.

1. Riah was a young Palestinian man living in a large city in the UK. He had been unemployed for a while, having been dismissed by his previous employer for voicing 'unacceptable political views' in the workplace. Riah was annoyed at the way he had been treated. He had not been advocating violence in any way but had simply been drawing attention to the plight of his people back in Palestine. He became so incensed at the building of the wall by the Israeli authorities that had carved his village into two that he decided to go on hunger strike. He was admitted to hospital, where the staff tried unsuccessfully to persuade him to break his strike.

2. Johann was on probation as a result of his violent temper and the way he had often been aggressive towards other people, especially when under the influence of alcohol. In his discussions with his probation officer, he often talked about injustices in the world, and the plight of Africa. He decided to go on a G8 protest march to express his strong views about global poverty. After completing the march, he got into an argument and a scuffle ensued and he was arrested.

3. Carol was staying in a women's refuge with her eight-year-old son following another violent attack upon her by her partner. Understandably her self-respect and self-confidence had taken a 'nose dive', but she refused to believe that all men were the same, as other women and some of the staff at the refuge were suggesting. She was appalled when, during a discussion she was verbally abused by other residents for expressing the hope that one day she would find another male partner she would be happy with. She began to feel that the atmosphere in the refuge was becoming oppressive towards her and her son, and she felt she had no alternative but to move out, even though she had not been able to make adequate arrangements.

4. Pedro and Simon lived together in a flat and were trying to 'make a go' of their relationship, even though they knew that other residents disapproved. They had applied to the local council adoption and fostering service to explore the possibility of fostering or adopting a child. They attended the group meetings and had begun to feel excited by the prospect, even though they had not yet received any formal confirmation that they would be accepted. After one group session, however, they were confronted by some of the other people who attended the sessions who forcibly expressed their disapproval of their behaviour and tried to warn them against attending any further sessions.

These examples illustrate ways in which competing, and at times clashing, value systems impinge upon the lives of people we work with. Sometimes, as in the case of Riah and Johann, some overriding concerns and a deep commitment to a wider set of values had a profound impact upon them and the life chances that were available to them. In other situations, it was other people's value systems that had a profound and negative impact.

A framework for evaluating various value systems
In this discussion we are not suggesting that all value systems are equal, nor that they are all necessarily good. Far-right extremist organizations, for example, could quite legitimately claim to have a value base that acts as a springboard for their policies and behaviour towards people of difference in our society. We therefore need some framework or benchmark by which to judge various value systems that people espouse.

For the purposes of our discussion, this framework is to be found in the theoretical concept of anti-discriminatory practice that was discussed earlier. This concept is based on the unique dignity and worth of every human being, and the understanding that the societies and communities in which we live can often be oppressive and discriminatory, thereby reducing our life chances and opportunities to thrive and be fully human. Therefore, we can use this in our work as a test by which to measure the attitudes and behaviours of others, especially towards people of difference and minority groups. If diversity and difference are both welcomed and celebrated, it allows individuals and groups to be themselves, to flourish and to contribute fully to the life of the community. If, on the other hand, their value base undermines and damages the individual dignity and worth of other people and refuses to facilitate the contribution that such people can make to the community, then it deserves to be challenged and rejected.

Class and religion
Earlier on in this discussion we included class and religion in the list of issues where the celebrating of diversity was important. We need to recognize that both of these issues can be 'used against' people in a discriminatory way. Some of the discussions about entry into higher education, and into the so-called elite group of universities, has focused on the lack of opportunities available to working-class students to break through into such institutions. Great attention has been paid to the efforts that these universities have made to create a much more level playing field and to remove the anomalies this approach seems to have created. The point being made here is that this is one example of where the issue of class is recognized as being significant.

The themes of religion and spirituality are another area that is coming under intense scrutiny. Within the mental health field, there is an increasing awareness that spirituality can be understood to have a much more positive and life-enhancing potential than had previously been acknowledged (Coyte *et al.*, 2008; Thompson, 2019). Spirituality is not particularly easy to define, but in recent literature there have been common themes associated with spirituality that involve the importance of finding meaning and purpose in life, in having resilience in the face of distressing and/or traumatic events and in having an enriched and enlarged worldview (Holloway and Moss, 2010). Unfortunately, the discussions in this area have tended sometimes to be oversimplified and become polarized into regarding spirituality as 'a good thing' and religion as 'a bad thing'. There are many examples where religion has stirred up fierce and bitter enmity and strife between people, communities and nations. While this is undoubtedly true, it is important to see both sides of the picture. There are some examples of spirituality that seem to foster only a self-centred narcissistic view of life that does nothing to support and care for others; and there are examples of religious devotion and allegiance that have led people to make enormous sacrifices on behalf of others, and to be committed tirelessly to the cause of social justice. So, it would appear that, in this area too, there is the potential for both good and evil, and the need to have a benchmark against which to judge and assess the effect of both religion and spirituality in people's lives.

The other important point to make is that, unless such allegiance can be demonstrably shown to be hurtful and destructive towards others, we should not be discriminating against people on these grounds. Therefore, whatever our personal views may be about Mormonism, Jehovah's Witnesses, Shamanism or paganism for example, we should not discriminate against those who espouse these worldviews just because they feel strange to us.

Reflective moment

Where does your spirituality come from? From a particular religion or faith community or from sources outside religion? What part do your values play in shaping your spirituality and what part does your spirituality play in shaping your values?

Conclusion

This discussion about celebrating diversity presents anyone working with people with a deep challenge if they are to achieve the gold standard of best practice. It is not a case of people workers somehow being outside the issues and pressures of what it means to be human and either male or female, young or old, disabled or non-disabled, straight or gay and so on.

We are people workers who bring to our work all the strengths and weaknesses, and possible prejudices, that have made us the unique individuals – male, female or otherwise – we have become. It is incumbent upon us, therefore, to be honest with ourselves and to realize that we have the potential to be just as discriminatory and oppressive in our attitudes as anyone else. Being professional does not exempt us from such territory; rather, it challenges us with the responsibility to be honest about them, to own them and then to deal with them, so that they do not get in the way of the work we are seeking to do with other people. And it is precisely to help us achieve this ideal that professional codes of practice and professional statements of values have such an important role to play. They provide the benchmark against which we can measure ourselves, our attitudes and our behaviour, so that those we work with can be confident that they will not be offered a second-class discriminatory service. The role of such codes of conduct is the subject of the next chapter.

Exercise 8
Why do many people find it difficult to value diversity and prefer to see differences between people as problems to be solved or dangers to be feared? What can be done to soften such attitudes and encourage a spirit of celebrating diversity?

Values at work

Introduction

We have emphasized that values-based practice is not simply a personal matter – values need to be understood in a broader cultural and structural context. But values also operate in an organizational context – that is, they are highly significant in the workplace. Consequently, in this chapter we explore the role of values in how organizations work (or fail to work), how individuals experience working life and how organizational problems arise.

Why work matters

The effects of being involved in paid work range across a spectrum from extremely positive and constructive to extremely negative and destructive. Positive experiences of work can bring immense satisfaction, enhance self-esteem, give a strong and helpful sense of identity, provide a sense of security and stability, a basis for helpful friendships and opportunities for growth, learning and personal development as well, of course, as a livelihood. People who are lucky enough to have a positive working life experience gain many benefits from it and this can also provide a better foundation for both physical and mental health (Bevan and Cooper, 2022; Ryan and Burchell, 2023).

By contrast, people who are unfortunate enough to be at the other end of the spectrum can find working life a set of major challenges and dissatisfactions, including such problems as stress, burnout, discrimination, bullying and harassment, conflict and aggression and violence. And, of course, the impact of these

DOI: 10.4324/9781003689614-10

can be highly detrimental in terms of physical and mental health, relationships, learning and development, self-esteem and confidence.

Just as the benefits of a positive working life can enhance life outside of work, work-related problems tend to have a knock-on effect for life outside of work. The negatives can unfortunately create vicious circles that can potentially reach catastrophic proportions. For example, someone who is highly stressed at work may take tensions home with them that have a detrimental effect on their family relationships and their ability to parent well. This can lead to family breakdown which can then add extra pressures on someone who is already struggling. This could lead to losing their job and thus another round of pressures and challenges.

The workplace is therefore not simply the physical location where (paid) work takes place; it also provides the emotional and spiritual context of people's lives and this, of course, brings values into the picture. It is therefore worth exploring the role of values in the workplace to see just how significant they are.

Values in the workplace

Workplaces are where people come together to achieve certain goals. There will be organizational goals, such as making a profit for a commercial organization or meeting citizen needs for a public service. But there will also be individual goals, not least to earn a living. These goals will reflect values, of course, and values can affect whether or to what extent the various goals are achieved. As we shall note below, there can be value conflicts that materialize in the workplace and certain work circumstances can lead to problem where people lose sight of their values because of the pressures they face.

Of course, people bring their own personal values to the workplace, but these are not the only ones that play a part in how the organization concerned operates. There will also be organizational values and professional values that can prove to be highly influential, sometimes in positive ways, but often in highly problematic ways.

Organizational values

Many organizations make their values explicit as part of their 'mission statement' that is, their statement about why the organization exists and what it is trying to achieve. However, such professed values are not necessarily actually used in practice. For example, there is no shortage of organizations that make values claims that they do not always live up to. This would include commercial companies that claim to be customer focused but regularly fail to listen to the customers or any concerns they may have. Likewise, various scandals about vulnerable people being abused in settings where they were supposed to be cared for have been numerous over the years. So, we need to recognize that espoused values, to use the technical term, are not necessarily the same as the actual values that underpin day-to-day practice.

Organizational values can also present difficulties in terms of different people interpreting them in different ways. For example, the value of treating people with respect may result in quite different behaviours or attitudes from a group of people who take respect and dignity seriously. This is often because of ingrained discriminatory assumptions or stereotypes. Someone working with older people who has not had training in relation to ageism, for example, may not realize that their actions and interactions or language use may actually be quite disrespectful if based on an ageist stereotype (see Thompson and Cox, 2025, for a discussion of ageist stereotypes and the harm they can do).

Professional values

Alongside organizational values we have professional values. In Chapter 10 we shall explore professional values in relation to various codes of practice and this will show how significant they are. However, what we need to do now is to acknowledge that, while different sets of professional values may have much in common, there will always be differences, especially of emphasis. For example, a community nurse who is concerned about an older person struggling to cope in the community may want a social worker to arrange for them to be admitted to a care home where they should receive the care they need. The social worker, while also wanting the older person to be safe, will have a value commitment to the older person's right to make their own decisions. If the older person does not want to give up their home and independence, however much of a struggle that is, then the social worker's value of self-determination will mean that they should not put them under pressure to make the decision either way.

Like organizational values, professional values can also be open to problems arising from differing interpretations of the same value. Confidentiality is a good example of this. You may have some people who adopt this value quite strictly, while others may not breach confidentiality fully but may bend the rules at times (with comments like: 'I shouldn't be telling you this, but I will if you promise not to breathe a word of it to anyone'). Such values can also be misunderstood or their full implications not appreciated. For example, one of the present authors (Neil) was once at a child protection case conference where a social worker explained that she could not comment on the content of the counselling that the child was receiving as this was confidential. She was quite right to say that, but she was subsequently criticized for breaching confidentiality as it was deemed that the very fact the child was receiving counselling was in itself confidential and had no bearing on the risk assessment the conference had been set up to discuss.

Reflective moment

Does the organization you work for (or are studying at) have explicit values? If so, are they actually evident in practice? Likewise, are you aware of what your professional values are and what they require of you?

Value conflicts

Values can come into conflict in a number of ways, not least the following:

Intrapersonal conflict

This refers to a value conflict that arises within the individual. It can happen in a number of ways:

■ A parent (or someone working *in loco parentis*) may experience a value conflict when, say, their teenager wants more independence and to be able to take more risks and thereby creates a clash between care and protection as a value and self-determination as an equally valid value, but one that does not sit comfortably with a desire to protect.

■ A person who was brought up in one culture but then moved at some point to another culture can feel conflicted in terms of the difficulties in reconciling two different sets of cultural values.

■ Similarly, someone brought up in a particular religious tradition may come to doubt, or even lose altogether, their faith. They may find then that their emerging personal values are at odds with the religious beliefs and values that they were raised in.

■ Intrapersonal conflicts can arise over political alliances. For example, someone committed to social justice may favour what is traditionally seen as a left-wing perspective. However, their experience of working in a large ineffectual state bureaucracy may lead them to lean in a more right-wing libertarian direction.

Interpersonal conflict

The point was made earlier that what is often seen as a clash of personalities is more likely to be a clash of values. For example, in the child protection field, before joint training for social workers and police officers was introduced, there was often conflict between the two professions, with the social worker focusing on supporting the child and family and the police officer focusing on securing a conviction. The joint training went a considerable way towards resolving this by emphasizing that the priority for both professions needed to be keeping the child safe.

Interpersonal conflicts are, of course, not limited to the workplace. Significant problems can arise when the tensions caused by workplace conflicts are taken home and into the community and vice versa. As tension can easily beget tension, there is a very real danger of a vicious circle developing. A useful way of preventing this is what is known as 'compartmentalization'. This involves trying to make sure that work tensions remain at work and home tensions at home, with a clear boundary between them. This can be difficult to do, but it is certainly worth making the effort.

Interprofessional conflict

Different professions can have different aims and emphases, as the child protection example above illustrates. Linked to this is the idea that different professions develop different cultures/cultural differences can manifest themselves in terms of differing values (of course), different traditions and variations in language use. In terms of language, the two main issues are the use of jargon and the level of formality ('register' to use the technical term). Jargon can be a very useful shorthand code provided that both parties are familiar with that code. Where one person uses technical terms or other forms of jargon that the other person is not familiar with, not only can communication break down, but also ill-feeling and resentment can arise, acting as a further obstacle to effective partnership and interprofessional collaboration. What can also be a problem is the fact that the same term can mean different things in different professional contexts. For example, the term referral can mean a request for a service (as used in health and social care), a recommendation (in a business context) or an assignment that did not meet the criteria for a pass mark (in education). The term 'assessment' is similarly ambiguous depending on the context in which it is used.

In terms of the level of formality, members of the legal profession (and, to a lesser extent, the police) are trained to use language quite precisely to avoid any future legal wranglings over how events or circumstances have been described or represented. This precision tends to make the language used more formal. By contrast, in a social care context, such formality can serve as an obstacle to building positive working relationships with service users and carers – it could be seen as 'standoffish'.

In working with fellow professionals, it is therefore important to be aware of differences in these cultures, especially in terms of the underlying values that are generally not made explicit.

Moral distress

This is a term used to describe situations where a person's work duties conflict with their values. In certain situations, a person seeking help or support from a particular organization may not meet the eligibility criteria to receive such help (their circumstances may be deemed to be of a not sufficiently severe level to warrant support being offered). A worker having to follow their employer's rules may experience moral distress in denying them a service while their strongly held value of compassion leads them to want to be helpful despite their organization's policy.

In some work contexts, moral distress can be a common situation where staff and managers motivated by compassion encounter situations where a shortage of resources prevents them from being helpful. Learning how to handle the frustration (and possible anger) associated with moral distress can be an important skill in some settings, especially in those areas where demands tend to outstrip supply.

Conflicting aims

In discussing interprofessional conflict earlier, we mentioned that there can be different aims or at least differing emphases. However, this is not the only way in which conflicting aims can create problems. A new member of a team may want to help the team to develop by drawing on insights gained from how things worked well in their previous team. Other team members may be focusing on helping the new team member to settle in and become 'acclimatized' to the culture of the team they have joined. This clash of focus can leave the new recruit feeling unwelcomed because their efforts to help are falling on stony ground, while the other team members feel patronized by the new member who they perceive to be criticizing how the team works.

Another example would be where a youth justice worker's aim is to prevent a young offender being incarcerated if they commit further offences, while the young offender's aim may be to get this representative of establishment authority off their back so that they do not lose status among their peers. Consequently, working practices can be significantly enhanced by clarifying respective aims and, where necessary, negotiating a positive way forward. This is the essence of partnership and, of course, a commitment to partnership working is a key professional value.

Key point

Some degree of conflict at times is inevitable. While wanting to avoid unpleasant conflict situations, a head in the sand approach can lead to situations getting significantly worse. Developing the skills and confidence to manage conflict effectively is a much wiser path to follow.

Exploitation or partnership?

N. Thompson (2025) draws a distinction between organizations that seek to exploit their employees to the full and those that aim instead to empower their staff to achieve the best results and to have the opportunity to learn, grow and flourish. This latter, more enlightened approach can be seen to be more beneficial for all concerned, although, despite this, the more traditional exploitative stance remains very common. The difference between the two approaches is largely a matter of values. An exploitative approach can lead to such problems as stress and burnout that we shall discuss below. Such situations arise from a lack of compassion and of a commitment to respect and dignity. Whether staff are treated as actual people with needs and feelings or simply as numbers on a staffing spreadsheet will largely determine how they respond, how motivated and engaged they are and how long they stay in post before looking for a better form of working life.

The key issue here is how the term 'human resources' is interpreted (Thompson, 2022). Employers who focus on the resources element and neglect the human side of the equation risk a wide range of problems (to be discussed below). By contrast, those employers who emphasize the human element are highly likely to find that staff become more resourceful and are therefore more productive and engaged and are likely to stay around longer and be more loyal. There is therefore a great deal to be gained by employers and employees alike if the way people are treated owes more to humanistic values than to simple expediency.

We have seen how partnership can in itself be seen as an important value. We should now be able to see that this applies just as much to the relationship between employers and employees as it does to the relationship between employee and client, customer, patient or service user. In a sense, partnership as a value represents the coming together of other values, such as compassion, respect and dignity and empowerment.

Workplace health and wellbeing

In recent years, there has been a major shift of emphasis towards a focus on workplace health and wellbeing, or 'employee wellness', as it is often called. Health and safety in the workplace have been significant concerns for many years, although, in practice, there has tended to be a much greater emphasis on safety than health. More recently, the health implications of working life have featured more strongly. It has been much more fully appreciated that, while there does need to be a focus on safety and the prevention of accidents, there are additional risks that relate specifically to health and, by extension, wellbeing (broadly defined as quality of life).

The health aspect involves recognizing and dealing with: (i) health hazards in the workplace (exposure to toxic chemicals, for example); (ii) the impact of health conditions on workplace practices (for example, in terms of infection and/ or an employee who is unwell practising at a suboptimal level and thus potentially dangerously); (iii) making reasonable adjustments for people with chronic illnesses or disabilities; (iv) supporting staff through periods of sickness absence and return to work; and (v) mental health concerns relating to stress, burnout, anxiety, depression and related matters.

Health and wellbeing are different entities, but they are related. Health status can affect quality of life and quality of life can affect health, both physical and mental health. The promotion of wellbeing has tended to focus on boosting the positives – improved sleep, diet and exercise, for example. However, what is also needed to develop a genuine culture of wellbeing is a commitment to addressing the negatives – tackling the obstacles to wellbeing, such as stress, burnout, bullying, discrimination and conflict. First, though, it is necessary to acknowledge that such problems exist and, unfortunately, many organizations do not. The values of honesty and openness therefore need to be called upon to make progress in this regard.

Underpinning a commitment to workplace health and wellbeing there need to be humanistic values, in the sense of, as we outlined earlier treating people *as people* – human resources and not just resources. Without this, there can be significant problems in terms of staff turnover and low levels of engagement. In our experience, many organizations struggle to maintain a full complement of staff. There are many reasons for this, but one clear feature of this situation is that employers cannot expect loyalty if staff do not feel valued, supported and safe. Similarly, people cannot realistically be expected to put their heart into their work if they feel that they are just a resource and not a flesh and blood person with wishes, feelings and needs.

It should be clear, then, that when it comes to the workplace, we need values-based practice in terms of how people are managed, supported and led as well as how staff relate to the people the organization serves. A people-centred approach to management that takes seriously employee wellness is therefore a fundamental basis for values-based practice.

The importance of leadership

When it comes to the role of values in the workplace, the key role of leadership needs to be recognized. An effective leader is someone who is clear about where the team and organization are trying to get to and what it is trying to achieve (the 'strategic vision', to use the technical term). To motivate staff to achieve that vision, it is essential that leaders articulate that vision well and make clear the values associated with that vision. For example, in a commercial organization, the value of customer care is likely to feature highly, while in, say, a social care setting, the value of providing care with dignity may be at the forefront. Clearly, then, values are a core part of leadership. Indeed, in our experience, where leadership fails to be effective tends to be those situations where either people in key positions have lost sight of their values or the values they bring to the workplace are not compatible with bringing out the best in people (for example, a competitive leader who tries to hold staff back rather than help them grow, develop and flourish). Workplaces where the values situation is problematic are often referred to as 'toxic' environments.

This is yet another reason why we need to be tuned in to values and try to make sure that values issues are part of the solution and not part of the problem.

Key point

Management and leadership can overlap in various ways, but they are not the same thing. It is possible to be a good manager but a poor leader and vice versa. Also, you do not have to be a manager to be an effective leader – it is possible (and quite common) for people to have a positive influence on the culture without being in a management role.

Conclusion

Work plays a significant role – for good or ill – in most people's lives. Problematic workplaces can have a knock-on effect on families and even, at times, communities. They can have an adverse effect on people's physical and mental health and their overall level of wellbeing and life satisfaction. Underpinning both the positives and the negatives of working life are values – especially those values associated with how we relate to one another.

Trust, respect, dignity, compassion, loyalty, honesty – these are all highly significant values that can make such a profound and far-reaching difference to how working life (and beyond) is experienced. Values-based practice is therefore not a matter simply for those staff engaged directly in working with customers, clients, service users or patients; it needs to be at the heart of all aspects of working life for everyone involved in the workplace if the best results are to be produced.

Exercise 9

Consider (i) an organization that you regard as a positive workplace and (ii) one that is problematic in a number of ways. What, in terms of values, makes the difference between the two?

Practising ethically

Introduction

In Chapter 8 we acknowledged the importance of ethical codes of conduct that control and direct the behaviours of the people workers who are employed by the various agencies to deliver a service to the community. The point was made that, if quality of service were left to the whim of the individual worker, there would be no guarantee of consistency throughout the agency, nor would the general public know what they could reasonably expect to receive when they went to the agency for help, advice or support. Codes of ethical conduct are therefore an important part of any value base for people work because they reflect a commitment to best practice and the valuing of each and every individual who comes to that agency. No one should receive a second-class service or be discriminated against, and one way of ensuring that the value base is operationalized is by having a code of conduct.

Such codes of conduct are not just aspirational, in that they set out what all workers should aspire to achieve (important though that is), they also serve as a benchmark against which conduct can be monitored and assessed. And this gives the public a measure of protection, in that they can take out a complaint against an agency or against one of its workers if they feel that the quality of service they have received has fallen short of what should be expected. Once again, this reflects a core element of the value base: each individual is important and deserves to receive the very best possible service from the agency and its workers, not least because of the partnership philosophy that was discussed in Chapter 5.

DOI: 10.4324/9781003689614-11

So far, we are likely to encounter little reaction against these observations. They are, we suggest, fairly uncontroversial and would find general acceptance among professional staff. The challenge is when we come to apply these general codes within a framework of multidisciplinary, interagency working, where different workers may have somewhat differing codes that govern how they might respond to someone who is using their services. To illustrate some of the richness, yet also complexity, of ethical codes of conduct, let us compare and contrast some familiar disciplines.

Exploring some codes of practice
In this chapter we explore some of the codes of practice for the range of people work being explored in this manual to help you gain some detailed understanding of the differences and similarities between them and their practice implications.

1. Social work
The British Association of Social Workers has issued a Code of Ethics for Social Work (BASW, 2014) that sets out three basic values to which social work is committed. These are:

- Human rights;
- Social justice; and
- Professional integrity.

Each of these values is then explored, and a set of principles established that are to guide the professional conduct of social workers as they work with those who use their services.

For example, human rights are presented in terms of human dignity and worth, as a value. This is understood to mean that every human being has an intrinsic value.

All persons have a right to wellbeing, self-fulfilment and as much control over their own lives as anyone else. This means that social workers have a duty to:

1. respect basic human rights as expressed in the United Nations Universal Declaration of Human Rights and other international conventions derided from that convention;
2. show respect for all persons and respect service users' beliefs, values, culture, goals, needs, preferences, relationships and affiliations;
3. safeguard and promote service users' dignity, individuality, rights, responsibilities and identity;
4. foster individual wellbeing and autonomy, subject to due respect for the rights of others;
5. respect service users' rights to make informed decisions and ensure that service users and carers participate in decision-making processes;

6. ensure the protection of service users that may include setting appropriate limits and exercising authority with the objective of safeguarding them and others.

A commitment to human rights echoes our important discussions earlier of the significance of rights and choice.

Professional integrity can be understood to include honesty, reliability, openness and impartiality, and, as such, is an essential value underpinning practice. This can be interpreted in the following terms:

Social workers have a duty:

a. to place service users' needs and interests before their own beliefs, aims, views and advantage, and not to use professional relationships to gain personal, material or financial advantage;
b. to ensure that their private conduct does not compromise the fulfilment of professional responsibilities and to avoid behaviour that contravenes professional principles and standards or that damages the profession's integrity;
c. to seek to change social structures that perpetuate inequalities and injustices, and whenever possible work to eliminate all violations of human rights.

This code of ethics applies to the UK only, but many other countries around the world have similar documents that explore similar themes, albeit with different wording and different emphases. There is, despite international differences, considerable consensus in terms of expected values (Thompson, 2016).

TIP! Don't think of a code of ethics as a set of rules to be followed unthinkingly. As we noted earlier, values are complex and 'slippery' hence the need for reflective practice to weigh issues up.

2. Medicine
Woodbridge and Fulford (2004) discuss the ethical code that doctors in the UK are expected to abide by, according to the General Medical Council:

1) make the care of the patient your first concern;
2) treat every patient politely and considerately;
3) respect patients' dignity and privacy;
4) listen to patients and respect their views;
5) give patients information in a way they can understand;
6) respect the rights of patients to be fully involved in decisions about their care;
7) keep your professional skills and knowledge up to date;
8) recognise the limits of your professional competence;
9) be honest and trustworthy;

10) respect and protect confidential information;

11) make sure your personal beliefs do not prejudice your patients' care;

12) act quickly to protect patients from risk if you have good reason to believe that a colleague may not be fit to practise;

13) avoid abusing your position as a doctor;

14) work with colleagues that best service the patients' interest.

(General Medical Council, 2004)

3. Nursing

Woodbridge and Fulford (2004) also discuss the professional code for nursing practice from the UK Nursing and Midwifery Council, which states that

> As a registered nurse, midwife or health visitor you are personally account-able for your practice. In caring for patients and clients you must:
>
> 1) respect the patient or client as an individual;
> 2) obtain consent before you give any treatment or care;
> 3) protect confidential information;
> 4) cooperate with others in the team;
> 5) maintain your professional knowledge and competence;
> 6) be trustworthy;
> 7) act to identity and minimise risk to patients and clients.

Comments on these codes

Woodbridge and Fulford (2004) observe that

> there are crucial differences of emphasis and even of detail. The nursing code, for example, although claiming to represent 'the shared values of all UK health care regulatory bodies' includes at least one value – 'cooperate with other members in the team' – which is absent from the other two codes. The other professionals would not necessarily disagree with this, but they do not actually mention it in their own codes.
>
> (p. 56)

Of course, the absence of a mention of a particular issue does not mean that the body concerned would not support its promotion. We cannot expect such documents to be comprehensive and exhaustive if they are to remain of a length and level of detail that is of practical worth on a day-to-day basis.

It would be useful to look at the code of conduct that you have for your own particular profession if it is different from the ones we have used as illustrative material for our discussion and undertake this 'compare and contrast' exercise in a similar way to how we have explored social work, medical and nursing codes in this chapter. They can be very revealing about professional expectations and how each profession sees its own role.

Key point

It is, of course, when we enter the arena of interprofessional collaboration that these issues become particularly complex, not least because each professional will have their own role that may or may not overlap to some extent with that of others who are involved. The question of how do such groups make their decisions and still work for the ultimate benefit of the people who rely in them for help is central for us all across the disciplines.

Power: Social work as a case example

The issue of power remains one of the key themes for anyone working in the human services, and it is implicit in all the codes of conduct that have been mentioned in our discussion so far. For social workers, the issue is at the forefront of their practice. This is because so often, and in so many ways, the people who rely on social work help are generally lacking in power for a number of reasons – mainly because of the disempowering consequences of discrimination and oppression.

As the codes of practice suggest, there is for social workers at least, an imperative to explore, identify and address (as far as they can) the issues of social injustice that so often disadvantage those members of the community they are engaged with in their professional practice. How social workers seek to tackle such issues takes us into the realm of power: how social workers exercise it and to what effect. There are admittedly constraints upon them: they are largely employees of a state organization and are ultimately accountable to their employers for their actions.

This is part of social work's location as 'stuck in the middle' between the (welfare) state that employs them and members of the community they serve (Thompson, 2016). For some people, however, this is overstating the issue. They would see social work to be much more of an agency that, first and foremost, contributes significantly to social cohesion and social stability. The work that a social worker will undertake with those who are disadvantaged will be essentially to ameliorate, where possible, the harsh impact that circumstances may have had upon them, and then to help them where possible to adjust effectively into society. This position may feel for some social workers to be more comfortable, in that it does not carry with it any expectation of seeking to effect change in any major way. On the contrary, the change is to be effective within the lives of individuals that are, for whatever reason, problematic – the skill of the worker lies precisely in helping that person or family begin to fit in more 'acceptably' with society.

Professional workers within the criminal justice system – prison officers and probation officers and those who work in youth offending teams – will immediately recognize the relevance of such an approach. The responsibility that society lays upon them can be understood precisely in terms of helping individuals change from a pattern of offending behaviour, which is by definition anti-social and detrimental to the common good, to more socially acceptable lifestyles in which houses are not burgled, cars not stolen or vandalized, and innocent people can go about their daily lives without fear of violence, assault or attack. The Home Office is very concerned to see crime rates reduced and looks to these human service professionals to play a major role in changing people's anti-social behaviour to a way of life that is more rewarding, both personally to the individual and to the community.

At one level, therefore, this is uncontentious. Indeed, it is one of the implications of the value base for society that seeks to respect everyone and accord them dignity and worth. If there are people who flout such values, then society has to have systems in place to deal with such situations if the fabric of society is not to be placed in jeopardy.

But, at a deeper level there are serious problems to be faced with this approach. If, as I would argue, society does not have such a unified and unifying consensus as is implied by the previous few paragraphs, then the picture is far less clear cut. If, as many would suggest, there are fault lines in the very structure of society that fundamentally disadvantage certain groups, then the whole question of consensus is under scrutiny, and the task of helping people adjust to a societal norm far more problematic.

This approach, of course, raises the question of whether social work is premised on empowerment or adjustment. If we settle for adjustment, which conveniently sidesteps the 'caught in the middle' dilemma, we then need to ask whether this can make social work a force for oppression, rather than for empowerment.

Consider the alternative view presented by Thompson (2024a, p. 24):

> According to this view, the recipients of social work help are predominantly members of oppressed minorities whose problems owe more to the structure of society than to their own personal failings or inadequacies. The task of social work, then, is to support the oppressed individuals, groups and communities in challenging the discrimination and inequality to which they are routinely and systematically exposed. This is an approach that is closely associated with what became known as 'radical social work', a perspective that emphasized the importance of working towards social change, rather than simply helping people adjust to their disadvantaged position.

This takes us back to the theoretical value base for our discussion outlined in Part One, particularly the chapter that explored the theme of anti-discriminatory practice. The basic premise of that approach argues that society does not treat everyone with equal dignity and respect, and until that day happens, it is incumbent upon social workers to strive actively to remove these inequalities. The central question then becomes not whether social workers have power, but how they exercise it and for whose benefit.

TIP! Don't be afraid of power. You would be of little use in your professional role if you had no power. The key issue is the *ethical* and responsible use of power.

Implications for other professionals

The discussion has focused upon social work because, in many ways, the issues can be seen most clearly there. But, this manual has a wider audience, and it is important to see ways in which these issues impinge upon the professional practice of others.

Advice workers, for example, are very familiar with this tension. Advisers who work for Citizens Advice, for example, have a long history of respecting the individual who comes to them for help with debt or benefits advice, or a wide range of other issues, and also keeping a record of particular issues that seem to crop up time and again, and that are seen to be disadvantaging their inquirers. As a result, the social policy arm of their work is precisely directed towards effecting change in society, by identifying and then campaigning for change. Far from being regarded as being in tension, both aspects of their work are seen as complementary and vital. Without this commitment to social change, their work would be an unending round of applying sticking plasters onto problems that will never be resolved.

Leaders of faith communities can also find themselves facing these issues in a very stark way. Their involvement with community issues often highlights the difficulties that poor housing, inadequate social and leisure provision, unemployment and poverty cause for the people in their direct or indirect care. This has led some (although by no means all) faith community leaders to campaign vigorously for social change and for an improvement in the life chances available to people 'on their patch' or in their parish.

Those who work with young people are often vividly reminded of the ways in which some young people are seriously disadvantaged, especially if they have been drawn into drug misuse, or have not achieved the level of academic attainment that will lead them easily into employment and career opportunities. 'Grown ups' (whoever they are!) often fail to understand the enormous societal pressures upon many young people and fail to see that personal and career success is not always a matter of willpower and determination, but needs at times a significant challenge to structures and attitudes before young people can have their potential recognized and released.

These examples from the many that could have been chosen highlight the issue of social change and roles that various people, including professional workers, can – indeed, must – play if the opportunities are to be available for disadvantaged people in our communities to become successful. And, to play that role, there will inevitably be the need for power to be used to effect change. And how that power is exercised will tell us a lot about the value base of the individual or groups exercising it.

One further point needs to be made. From this discussion it will be clear that every worker will have positioned him- or herself somewhere on this spectrum that ranges from a consensus view of society into which we are seeking to help 'misfits' (to put it crudely) adjust, to the view about society that sees it as being flawed and discriminatory, with the result that professional workers understand their role to include a drive towards social justice. There is, however, no neutral value-free hiding place – professional workers are either part of the solution or they become part of the problem (Thompson, 2021).

Challenging inequality

Much of this chapter has explored this theme already, particularly in the discussion about how power can be used either to help ameliorate people's life chances or to increase the impact of discrimination or oppression. This was summed up in the idea that professional workers are either part of the solution or they become part of the problem.

As a statement of intent, 'challenging inequality' seems uncontentious. Indeed, in the context of our discussion that seeks to recognize the intrinsic value and dignity of each individual, the aspiration to remove any obstacle that prevents such a recognition should not provoke any violent disagreement.

The difficulty comes in trying to define what the mirror image of this concept means. How clear a picture do we have about equality, which we presume is the state to which our aspirations to challenge inequality are leading us? It is here that we begin to encounter some difficulties. In his detailed discussion of these themes, Thompson (2018a) reminds us that: 'being equal does not necessarily mean being the same ... a better understanding of difference and diversity is an important part of promoting equality' (p. 7).

Key point

Equality should not be interpreted literally to mean sameness. It is about equal fairness and being free from unfair discrimination.

Thompson's observation takes us to the heart not only of what professional people work is all about, but also of how we understand and shape the society we live in. Of course, there remains a strong element of challenging inequality in all its guises, even though sometimes it takes a major catastrophe to reveal exactly what a society or community is like. The tragic aftermath of the Hurricane Katrina in 2005 that flooded an area the size of the UK and reduced huge swathes of New Orleans and the surrounding areas to pulverized driftwood, had a number of sombre messages. But one unavoidable conclusion was that those who could not get into a car to escape the hurricane, and those who had most to lose, were predominantly the black community who for the most part were desperately poor and literally had nowhere else to go. Political commentators began to wonder whether the response to such a catastrophe would have been far more swift and comprehensive had the hurricane decimated a more affluent area.

The point being made here is not an idle speculation about what the US Government could or should have done differently. Rather, it illustrates that in this disaster the true nature of inequality within that area was revealed for what it was. Natural disaster is no respecter of wealth, privilege or position – but those who are socially advantaged often have greater resources and opportunities to emerge more successfully than those who are socially disadvantaged.

Within the context of professional people work, we are beginning to be aware that there is a richer and more comprehensive dimension to the discussion than we had previously recognized. For some time now, as we discussed in Chapter 5, the equality, diversity and inclusion movement has played a seminal role in challenging inequality and ensuring that legislation is introduced that makes discrimination on various grounds illegal. The importance of these developments cannot be underestimated: they reflected the value base being argued for in this manual and helped to reshape public opinion in key areas, such as race, gender, age and disability. What perhaps was missing from this debate was a vision of what society could become, and a celebration of the values that underpin this vision.

This is why, in recent years, the emphasis has been more upon diversity and celebrating diversity. It is not enough to produce a legal framework: society has to own and celebrate the value base that it seeks to live by. And, as we have seen in our discussion about anti-discriminatory practice, there are fundamental challenges to this value base running through society. It is going to take more than some legal adjustments, however crucial these may be, to reach the situation where everyone in the community is not only valued and treated with dignity, but where their differences and diversity are celebrated as an enrichment to the community that otherwise would be immeasurably the poorer.

This theme also explores the importance of creating, developing and maintaining valued social roles for people in their communities. However we may try for ourselves and for those with whom we work to cultivate and develop a sense of value for who we are, there remains the reality that it is most often the things we do that bring to us a greater sense of wellbeing. If we have a sense that we are important to others, and are relied upon in some ways, and have a key role to play in an organization, however small that role may be, then our own sense of self-worth is likely to be enhanced.

> **Key point**
>
> There is an important link with the idea of partnership working that we explored earlier. If we take over and deny the possibility of people doing anything for themselves, we diminish even further their self-worth and ability to believe in themselves.

That process of helping people believe in themselves and recover from whatever has brought them to a low ebb is another major theme in the value base of people work, to which we now will turn in Chapter 11.

Exercise 10
Review the Code of Ethics or equivalent that governs your particular professional background. How confident are you that your practice is consistent with it? Is there anything that you can do to use such a code to improve your practice?

Promoting recovery

Introduction

Mental health problems are a common challenge across the people professions in family, community and workplace settings. The medical model that seeks to understand such problems narrowly as symptoms of an illness continues to be challenged and criticized for oversimplifying complex, multidimensional phenomena by reducing them to issues of biological malfunctioning (Kirk *et al.,* 2015; Thompson, 2019).

How we perceive and understand mental health problems is in large part a matter of values. In particular, what we have seen emerge is an emphasis on *recovery*, the ability of people struggling with mental health challenges to return to a state of far-improved wellbeing. In this chapter, we therefore explore the values issues involved in a recovery approach to mental health.

Why mental health? Why recovery?

We need to stress that all people workers in whatever agency or discipline they work, need to have at very least a basic awareness of mental health issues and the impact that mental distress can have upon the people who use their services.

This caveat is important because of the key word 'recovery' that features so strongly here. Recovery is a crucial concept in current mental health theory and practice and remains at the heart of the Department of Health's approach. As such, it encapsulates the value base of much mental health work.

At the heart of this concept is the belief in the capacity of an individual to move beyond and out of the control of whatever condition may have temporarily

DOI: 10.4324/9781003689614-12

upset their emotional, even physical wellbeing. With the help and support of relevant and significant 'others' – friends, family, mental health professionals, and at times with the support of appropriate therapeutic interventions – individuals learn to respond adaptively and creatively, and to develop the skills and capacity to recover from whatever circumstances had been disabling them.

The concept of recovery is also very relevant to trauma-informed practice (Walsh and Thompson, 2019). In recent years, there has developed a major emphasis on recovery from trauma, especially childhood trauma, and the notion of adverse childhood experiences (or ACEs) has become widely used in relation to adult mental health problems. There is now a significant body of evidence making strong links between childhood trauma and later mental health challenges (Bellis *et al.*, 2014). This increasing emphasis on traumatic experiences highlights further the importance of recovery.

This belief in the capacity of people to change and achieve recovery is an important challenge to those who may assume that a label is for life. This position assumes that, once a person has been 'diagnosed', shall we say, as 'manic depressive' or as 'schizophrenic', then that remains their single most important characteristic. No matter what life chances may subsequently come their way, it will be this label that exercises the most powerful influence, not least with potential employers. Such labels give out strong messages about their capacity to contribute to society: there will always be an inherent hesitation and uncertainty about whether they have the ability to fulfil what a job demands of them, and they will always be perceived as having diminished potential. To put it bluntly, they will always carry the stigma wherever they go.

It is fundamentally to challenge these labels, stereotypes and stigmatizing attitudes that the concept and practice of the 'recovery model' has been introduced within mental health practice. The person is always greater than the label that others attach: the capacity that individuals have to contribute to the wellbeing of others and society is never wholly obliterated. There will, of course, be occasions when a person's capacity is temporarily blunted, and when the contribution that they make will be more of a passive than active one, as they draw out from others a measure of compassion and concern. But the intrinsic value of that individual remains unsullied, and there must always remain the belief that recovery is possible, and that their dignity and value remain unquestioned.

Key point

Recovery is an important concept for all human service workers, but we must use the concept with care and always remember that its principal meaning has been drawn from the sphere of mental health where the value base of the term has a particular resonance. But, other fields of people work can also lay claim to it.

Recovery: An example from practice

Advice workers, for example, will be very familiar with scenarios where people come to them for help and support because they are overwhelmed by a mountain of debt or similar seemingly insuperable financial problems. The advice worker has an immediate responsibility to take stock of the problems being presented, decide on the priorities and urgent matters, and where necessary, begin to take some immediate action at least to achieve a 'holding position' to ensure that things do not get worse, and/or that the enquirer does not lose their home. From there on in, however, the value base of partnership working begins to take effect and the worker will be at pains to ensure that the enquirer's capacity to take responsibility for future actions is kindled and nurtured.

Dependency is the last thing that the enquirer wishes to foster. On the contrary, a successful outcome will be a situation where the person in debt 'recovers' their capacity to plan their financial circumstances more effectively – perhaps even to 'recover' their sense of direction and purpose in their lives that had become submerged beneath the debt mountain. It may well take time before they get back onto an even keel; life may never be the same again in some ways. But to the extent that they feel that they are back in charge of their lives, and that they are controlling the direction they are taking, then to that extent they may be described as on the road to recovery.

There is a further dimension to this in parallel with the mental health framework within which the concept of recovery has been established. It is not unusual for a person who has recovered from mental distress that had debilitated them for a period of time to have had a risk assessment undertaken in partnership with the professional worker who had been assigned to them. This assessment might well have highlighted certain factors that led to the onset of the problems, and which would need to be avoided, or at least controlled, if a recurrence of the situation is to be prevented. Stress factors are a good example of this. Being human, we all have our vulnerabilities, and one major factor in recovery is the acknowledgement of our individual vulnerabilities and the factors that can sap our self-confidence and sometimes our mental wellbeing. Recovery therefore does not have cast-iron guarantees – the possibility of relapse is always a risk. There is a continuing responsibility upon each one of us to cherish our wellbeing by studiously remembering what can overwhelm us and practising those disciplines of mind and body that offer us some protection against relapse. Recovery, therefore, (not to put too fine a point on it) is a precious gift that celebrates our value and worth, but must never be taken for granted, either by the individual involved or by any professional worker who happens to be working with them in the future, for whatever reason.

TIP! Beware of the tendency, reinforced by the dominance of the medical model, to focus narrowly on biological matters and thereby fail to take account of wider issues.

To return to our advice work example for a moment, we can sketch in a similar scenario. It is perfectly possible for any recovery to be short lived. The enquirer may express profuse gratitude to the advice worker that the immediate mountain of debt and its profound consequences have been ameliorated; the debt may have been significantly reduced, the threat of eviction removed, and a light now glows at the end of the tunnel. However, if there have not been significant changes in both the external circumstances and, importantly, in the worldview and mindset of the enquirer, they may be knocking at the adviser's door six months later with a repeat of the original problems. Recovery will have been almost a fantasy – a fleeting moment of relief before the reality bites even more deeply.

In order for recovery to be long lasting, the enquirer will need to have developed strategies not only for paying back the priority debts, but also to have taken a serious decision about whether a debt lifestyle is going to characterize the future. The risk factors will need to be identified; the vulnerabilities recognized and strategies put in place to counteract what has clearly become a major issue in that person's life. It will be vital to acknowledge that this is not a matter of individual pathology – the debt is not that person's fault entirely. We live in a society where debt is actively encouraged, and where societal pressures upon many people are enormous. So, it is hardly surprising that so many people find themselves in precarious situations financially. What will make all the difference to a particular individual's 'recovery' in these circumstances will not be a societal change (debt will always be with us and the encouragement to borrow will remain intense); nor entirely a change in the individual's circumstances (though debt remission and repayment terms that are manageable are crucially important). What will make all the difference is the attitude of the person concerned, and the determination to take responsibility to sustain the changes that have contributed to the recovery, so that the return into debt can be avoided, if at all possible.

This example illustrates once more the importance of the values debate that this manual is seeking to address. If the advice worker works from a value base that does not respect the individual, acknowledge the serious impact of societal forces on individuals or recognize – let alone cherish and work with – the potential for change, the chances of recovery will be slim. If, on the other hand, the value base of the worker is grounded in a partnership approach that seeks to value and empower the individual and refuses to pathologize what are often cultural and/or structural problems, then the potential for recovery is immeasurably enhanced.

Acknowledging risk

This chapter has explored the important concept of recovery, and has suggested that, with a degree of care, it can play a useful part in identifying an important aspect of the value base of people work. Of key importance is the conviction that people and their circumstances can change for the better, and that a people worker's value base can play a significant role in recognizing, cherishing and facilitating this change. Equally important, however, is the following caveat: all change brings with it a health warning! Unless an adequate risk assessment has been undertaken and people learn actively to guard against and counteract the factors that brought them (perhaps) near to despair, they could quickly lose their recovery and find that it was a passing, transient moment. There are no absolute guarantees of success.

This chapter has explored a concept that goes not only to the heart of the value base of people work but also uncovers something of what we believe it means to be human. It raises important questions about how we treat each other, especially in times of difficulty. All of these issues are part and parcel of the values foundation that underpins all people work.

Hope

Admittedly this concept does not appear too often in the glossary section of core texts used by a wide range of human services practitioners. It is none the less central to the value base of much of the work we undertake and, we would argue, is implicit in the value base we are discussing.

Many examples can be cited from a wide range of people work where individuals who are going through a particular set of difficulties frequently use the phrase 'it's hopeless'. Ground down by the apparent impossibility of what they are having to face, it is understandable that a deep pessimism ensues, and the future appears to be without hope.

The response that a worker makes to such a claim is important, not least because an inappropriate response runs the risk of exacerbating the feelings being experienced by the person the worker is seeking to engage with. A cheery 'Come on now, it can't be that bad!' type of response is rarely likely to have the desired effect.

On the contrary, it may simply confirm that the worker has not got a clue as to how the person is really feeling. Basic listening skills warn us against such a cavalier and superficial response. If, however, we can begin to appreciate really how that person is feeling and can spend time getting inside the range of difficulties that is causing that person to be so pessimistic about their future, then there is a chance that we might be able to begin to effect some change – although here too there are no guarantees! The difference in this approach is that the people worker is working from a strong value base that fundamentally respects the person being worked with and does not seek to minimize or devalue the problems that have brought them to their moment of despair. It is only when such moments can be acknowledged and a person's dignity respected that a way forward can at least be contemplated.

In other words, hope is not a commodity that can be transferred from the worker to the person using our services in a mechanistic way. The worker's own hope remains just that – the worker's. Hence the frequent retort: 'It's all right for you to say that – you're not in the mess I'm in'. The worker has a more difficult challenge, and that involves so valuing and respecting the person going through the difficulties that a sense of being 'believed in' begins to take root and begins to liberate the capacities to cope that had previously been overwhelmed. In such an encounter, the seeds of hope are planted, and the skill of the worker will be to nurture the faint glimmering of hope and facilitate the client to begin to claim and own it for themselves.

Conclusion

This chapter has explored the important concept of 'recovery' that we have argued can be applied to a much wider set of scenarios than the mental health setting that has given it a particular emphasis. Any human services practitioner should be able to explore the extent to which, as a result of their help and intervention, a person is able better to cope in the future and embark upon a journey that has begun to be tinged with hope, not least because a degree of empowerment has been achieved as a result of the worker's help. To the extent that that objective has been reached, a worker may rightly feel that their professional value base has been effective.

The discussion has also raised the issue of each individual's capacity to change, and the extent to which a worker really believes that people have strengths that can be released and harnessed to good effect to support and sustain creative change. It is to this crucial theme that we next will turn.

Exercise 11

Recovery is a useful concept for understanding situations where a person's life has taken one or more significant turns for the worse and where attempts are being made to return to a more positive position (hence its use in mental health work). In what ways can a recovery approach be applied to the type of work you are involved in? How might you use it?

Identifying people's needs and strengths

Introduction

One of the problems of being professional people workers is that, as a result of training and experience, a sense of 'knowing best' can begin to set in. Of course, in some ways, this is both largely inevitable and a cause for celebration. It is a source of profound relief that we do not have to reinvent the wheel with every encounter. Indeed, we pay certain individuals to develop and practise expertise, in medical and legal matters, for example, so that it will be available to people when they need it. Many aspects of people work involve sharing with those who come for help the benefits of our knowledge, our familiarity with 'the system' and how to make it work to that person's advantage.

At a deeper level, however, the feeling that we know best can have a debilitating impact upon the people we work with. Colleagues involved in working with young people know all too well that any attempt to impose the worker's worldview or value base upon a young person is likely to be met with a very robust challenge. We are back in the same territory that we were exploring earlier – that of respecting each individual and seeking to understand their point of view and their choice of lifestyle. Perhaps their choices have led them into some confusion or difficulty; perhaps they have found themselves clashing with society's expectations about what it means to live in the same community as others; perhaps they secretly want to make changes to their lifestyle. The key to all of this, however, is the ability of the worker first and foremost to respect the dignity and individuality of each person they work with, and to give them time and attention to demonstrate that they are unique and important as people.

DOI: 10.4324/9781003689614-13

As part of that attention giving, there is the important theme of acknowledging that each and every individual has strengths and capacities that may from time to time be negated by the awfulness of the problems they face but are never totally obliterated. This is a central conviction within the value base of all people work and deserves some discussion.

Part of the 'I know best' approach that can overtake people workers is the preoccupation with the problems that beset the particular individual they are working with. As the examples we have already cited clearly show, these can indeed be overwhelming and often deserve immediate attention if the person is not to be totally disempowered. But the person is always greater than the problem, and one of the fundamental aspects of the value base of the people worker is to acknowledge this and to be looking constantly for the signs of the individual's strengths and resilience that will need to be brought into play if the problems are not to have the final say. This means that the role of the people workers is not to solve someone else's problems for them, but rather to work in partnership with them in order to recognize, release and maximize the potential and strength they have for living their lives successfully.

We must admit, however, that there is a temptation in much people work, not only for the worker to think that they know best, but also to work with a 'deficit model' in seeking to understand those who use their services. This 'deficit model' goes something like this:

> We (the professional workers) are strong, capable, insightful, well-trained, resourceful, able to solve problems, and to be successful helpers. You (the person using our services/client) by contrast, are weak, unable to solve your problems, lacking insight, somewhat helpless, and therefore so fortunate to have us to work with you to give you the benefit of our skills and knowledge, so that some measure of improvement can be achieved in your mediocre lives.
>
> (Moss, 2005, p. 74)

If we are honest, we will all recognize the temptation to fall back on the deficit model in our professional practice. But, simply to overstate it by using the above quotation in this way points up its inherent arrogance, and the different value base it is premised on.

By contrast, the values that we are extolling in this manual as the foundation for best practice in people work would seek to underline the importance of a strengths perspective in our approach. As Hodge (2003, p. 14) observed:

> This framework posits clients' personal and environmental strengths as central to the helping process ... without a reliable means for finding clients' strengths, practitioners tend to revert to practice models that are based upon the identification of problems and deficits.

Much of the discussion from Chapter 11 is relevant to this issue, so we will not repeat it. Instead, taking those points raised previously as read, we want to introduce an additional theme that illuminates and enriches this notion of strengths.

Resilience

There is a growing literature on the theme of resilience that is helpful to explore at this point. As with the discussion on recovery, so too with resilience, we can approach this from both a narrow and wider perspective.

Resilience as a concept owes much to the work of Rutter (1999) who explored the complex and fascinating territory of abused children. Rutter sought to identify factors that predispose some abused children to rise above their damaged personal history and to lead successful and fulfilled lives, whereas others 'go under' and find that their history determines their future to an unacceptable and disempowering degree. In his discussion, he argues that it will be those children who are able either to incorporate their experience and understanding of adversity into their existing worldview, or alternatively who can reshape their worldview in order to bring some greater sense of meaning into it, who will likely to be more resilient and able to cope with further adversity. Rutter goes on to argue that:

> For psychologically healthy adult development and relationships, people need to accept the … reality of the bad experiences they have had, and to find a way of incorporating the reality of these experiences into their own self-concept, but doing so in a way that builds on the positive while not denying the negative.
>
> (p. 135)

The idea of a worldview that we all choose is an important aspect to this discussion. Our worldview will be constantly at work, trying to make sense of what happens to us. The more we are able, to follow Rutter's point, to discover and 'own' a satisfying worldview, the more fulfilled we are likely to be as people. Furthermore, we are more likely to be able to discover (or rediscover) our strengths and capacities when events happen that challenge the view of the world that we hold. Resilience therefore becomes a vital capacity of being human and is something that we need to be seeking to foster and deepen in the people we are working with and who are often struggling to find meaning in some distressing and bewildering events that befall them.

Once again, it is not the worker's role to seek to persuade the person using our services to take 'on board' the worker's own chosen worldview to make sense of what happens in the world. Rather, it is open to the worker to explore with that person their own worldview and how the events that are bringing them to the worker for help are to be seen within that framework. Within such explorations the seeds of resilience are sown, and within such frameworks an individual's strengths can be recognized and drawn out. In other words, the worker is operating from a value base that sees the person using the services, not the worker, as the ultimate 'expert' in that person's lifestyle and life choices.

Thompson and Cox (2020) point out that most of the literature on resilience is individualistic and psychological in its focus, paying little or no attention to the range of wider social factors that also play a part. This alerts us to the need to avoid adopting too narrow a perspective on resilience and take account of the social issues we have been discussing (power, discrimination and so on).

Key point

If we see resilience as a quality of the individual, rather than see it more holistically as a phenomenon that owes much to wider contextual factors, we run the risk of slipping back into a deficit model that pathologizes individuals who struggle to achieve resilience because of the adverse circumstances they find themselves in.

Spirituality

This discussion about our worldview opens up the fascinating panorama of the contemporary debate about spirituality. Admittedly, the very word 'spirituality' causes some people's hackles to rise because, for them, it smacks too much of the supernatural and religious systems to which they do not subscribe. Others, by contrast, who feel at home in a faith community of their choice, feel that this is a term they are very familiar with and welcome its arrival in the contemporary debate with unalloyed enthusiasm, feeling that they have some measure of ownership of the term.

We need to admit, therefore, at the outset that, while there is for some people an overlap between religion and spirituality, for others the term has meaning and resonance because it seems to capture something of the search for meaning and purpose that is at the heart of being human. While some find that meaning in the existence of a divine being and a life lived in worship and service, others use the word spirituality to capture and express some of the indefinable qualities and aspects of being human, without needing a supernatural context in which to understand them. They nevertheless feel that the word 'spirit' (however difficult it may be to define) both captures, and points to, an important facet of being fully human.

Although this is not the place for a detailed discussion on these themes, it is nevertheless important to recognize that, in a range of people work, issues to do with religion and spirituality are frequently ignored or subsumed under an awareness of a person's cultural needs. And yet, for many people, a religious framework (albeit undefined) continues to have some significance. In the 2021

Census in England and Wales, 46.2 per cent of the population identified as Christian and 6.5 per cent identified as Muslim. (https://www.ons.gov.uk/peopl epopulationandcommunity/culturalidentity/religion/bulletins/religionenglanda ndwales/census2021)

Leaving aside various other faith communities, and the fact that it may be very difficult to get to know precisely what these labels and allegiances mean to each individual, it nevertheless places these issues centre stage as far as a lot of people work is concerned. Put starkly, these statistics suggest that, for many people we work with, there may well be a religious dimension of sorts to their lives, and possibly also a source of resilience and strength that comes from that worldview. Certainly also (for a minority) resilience and strength come from belonging to a faith community that is supportive and encouraging, especially in times of difficulty and crisis, and in providing them with a worldview that is satisfying to them, even in times of deepest crisis or need.

> **TIP!** Don't make the mistake of assuming that spirituality applies only to religious people. Everyone has spiritual needs and faces spiritual challenges, regardless of their attitude to religion.

But the debate is wider than this. For many people who do not subscribe to a faith system, the concept of spirituality is still important, in that it provides a channel for their thinking and articulation of those (sometimes indefinable) issues that give meaning, purpose, enrichment and enchantment to their lives. However uncomfortable the term may be to some, the issues to which it points are central to the experience of being human. And, if major crises and difficulties cause us to think again about the worldview we have chosen to adopt, then implicitly if not always explicitly, spirituality comes onto our agenda, and therefore onto the agenda of any professional people worker we may go to in times of difficulty or crisis.

We are suggesting, therefore, that best practice in people work will always seek to look beyond the immediacy of the problems and crises that cause people to seek our help and support and be open to exploring issues of strengths and resilience that are often the key to whether or not a person will 'ride the storm'. For some, that key will have a religious dimension to it; for everyone, including those who vehemently deny the validity of any religious perspectives, the issue of spirituality can be a rich and rewarding exploration of meaning and purpose that will have a great impact upon an individual's strength, capacity and resilience to cope.

Supporting a variety of lifestyles

One further theme deserves discussion in relation to the value base we work from, namely the extent to which we can support people in a range of lifestyle choices. That this is a key question may be illustrated from just a few examples. In whatever aspect of people work you undertake, try to answer the following questions:

1. Would you support a request from a learning-disabled couple in a residential setting who wish to share a room and a sexual relationship?
2. A gay couple wish to apply for adoption, which is a legal possibility. But for you, to what extent is their sexual orientation an issue? Would your views change depending on whether the couple were female or male?
3. How would you respond to a young person you are working with who refuses to stop using cannabis for recreational purposes while on a group orienteering project in the Lake District for a week under your leadership?

These three examples from the many we could have chosen illustrate some of the dilemmas facing workers and the complex issues that often arise when making decisions. The reason for choosing these three is that each of them has a wider dimension than the individual's lifestyle choices. Individual lifestyles impact upon others, directly or indirectly, and as workers we need to keep these perspectives in mind and explore the implications with the people concerned. One of the guidelines we need to use is whether an individual's lifestyle choice is likely to affect the safety and wellbeing of others. Another is whether there is any clash with the law.

Reflective moment

We can feel quite unsettled or even threatened when asked to deal with situations that do not fit our own value positions. So, what value conflicts over lifestyle choices might you encounter? Forewarned is forearmed.

Conclusion

What we have seen in this chapter is that it can be easy, especially when we are under pressure from other people to do so, to slip into a 'we know best' mentality that can unwittingly devalue and disempower the people we are trying to help. We therefore need to focus not only the needs, problems and challenges people face, but also the strengths and resilience factors that can play such an important role if we remember to take them into account.

In much of the discussion so far it has been clear that we have placed the people we serve centre stage in our thinking and deliberating, and that this is a vital aspect of the value base of our work. The next chapter makes this theme crystal clear.

Exercise 12

How can you identify a person's strengths? What sorts of questions might you be able to ask? What other evidence of strengths and resilience might you be able to find?

Providing person-centred care

Introduction

Our previous discussions on recovery in Chapter 11 highlighted the ways in which this concept can be applied to many more helping professionals than just in mental health. The same holds true for this chapter: all the issues have a far wider relevance, and have important things to say not only about the process and procedures that professional people workers implement (which is not the theme of this manual), but also the value base that is implicit in them (which *is* the theme of this manual).

In this area above all there is the temptation we discussed earlier for the professional to think they know what is best for that person and to use their professional authority, power and influence to impose their views, however charitably intended, upon the person concerned. It is often not at all easy for a client to challenge what is being said by the professional – indeed, it is often much easier to smile, agree, say thank you and leave, rather than admit to not being able to tackle the tasks that the professional has so persuasively set for them to undertake before the next appointment. To get that right involves an important skill; it is also an important aspect of the value base of the work that is being undertaken.

To be clear, then, what we mean by person-centred care is practice rooted in a commitment to putting the client at centre stage. This may sound obvious, but what we often find is that practice, instead of being person centred, can be:

- *Budget centred*: Financial issues can override the needs of the individual. Of course, budgets will always be limited, and not all needs can be met, but

DOI: 10.4324/9781003689614-14

when we put the budget first – rather than trying to balance budget pressures and individual needs – we risk practising unethically.

- *Workload centred*: Of course, workload pressures have to be managed but failing to focus on a person's needs because we 'are busy' is highly problematic. It can amount to fobbing someone off to ease the pressures on us, rather than listen properly.

- *Administration centred*: We can sometimes be caught in the middle between bureaucratic pressures and clients' needs. Again, this is something that needs to be managed, not avoided by giving in to administrative pressures at the expense of people's needs.

- *Service centred*: Sadly, despite the long-standing emphasis on needs-led assessment, rather than service-led, it seems that many people still allow service availability to dictate their response, rather than looking creatively and holistically at meeting needs.

An example from practice

To illustrate this, let us return to the example used earlier of the advice worker trying to help the person overwhelmed by debt. We argued that the enquirer is likely to be feeling pessimistic about their future, with their self-confidence having taken a serious knock. From the advice worker's point of view, there is an important balance to be achieved between two equally disabling and disempowering approaches. The first would be to take all responsibility and action away from the enquirer. This carries the subtext that the worker feels that the enquirer is 'hopeless' and has not got a clue about how to proceed, a message that the enquirer quickly picks up and uses to confirm their own temporary assessment of themselves. The second would be to give the whole burden back to the enquirer with a lot of tasks to be done, a cheery pat on the back and a jovial encouragement for them 'to let us know how you get on'. The end result would be to leave the enquirer as depressed as before – perhaps even worse, because the hoped-for help had not yielded any tangible results.

The skill of the adviser will rest in their ability to establish a trusting relationship with the enquirer, and to prioritize what needs to be done, and then to negotiate achievable and meaningful goals for each of them to attempt before the next appointment. This may in fact lead to an initial apparent imbalance of tasks, with the worker tackling some of the high-priority matters, and the enquirer having a much more modest task to achieve by next time. At this stage the crucial issue is whether the tasks that have been negotiated for the enquirer have been honestly discussed and mutually agreed as being achievable.

In some ways this is no more and no less than the answer to the famous question: How do you eat an elephant? The answer: one mouthful at a time! The key to a successful outcome lies not only in having an overall strategy for tackling the problems (for which the worker is likely to be taking the lead at first), but in breaking down the necessary tasks into small enough bite-sized chunks for the enquirer to undertake successfully.

> **Key point**
>
> The key term when it comes to goal setting is *achievable*. Agreeing goals that the enquirer is going to struggle with is to set them up to fail, with the likely result that confidence is further eroded, rather than built up.

As the process towards recovery continues, so the balance between worker and enquirer will change, perhaps subtly at first, but soon in a dramatic fashion as confidence and resilience are regained. In the end, the test of a successful outcome will be the extent to which the enquirer has not only responded creatively to the tasks suggested by the helper but has also taken back ownership and control over the whole situation and has gained in confidence and insight to modify their lifestyle to avoid getting into similar difficulties again. This is empowerment in action. This, of course, may feel like a perfectionist's wish list! In the real world, workers proclaim, it is not like that at all – progress is much more erratic; people don't always get it right the second time; they don't always want to take responsibility and will be far happier if someone else takes over for them, and 'sorts it'.

Of course, this is true! Every people worker reading this manual will have abundant examples of this sort of situation where progress is at best chequered – what Schön (1983) called 'the swampy lowlands' of practice. The point about this, however, is not to deny the reality of this, but to re-emphasize the central importance of the value base of our work. The more times it takes to help people arrive at a commonly agreed objective, the more important it is to maintain the same value base at each and every attempt.

Again, let us return to our example. At the second interview, let's assume that the worker has achieved their objectives, and that the repossession of the house has been put 'on hold'. But, the enquirer comes back sheepishly to report that the seemingly simple task of finding further documentary evidence of what bills are outstanding has not been achieved. The worker's response at this point will be critical. If they go into omni-competent mode, and implicitly or explicitly gives a message to the enquirer that they can't be trusted, even with the most simple tasks, then the enquirer's already low self-confidence will be further reduced; helplessness will be increased and, from both the worker's and enquirer's perspective, there will come the whispered response: 'I told you so!'

This would be a self-fulfilling prophecy. The only way to break out of it would be for the worker to maintain the value base that underpins the work and to talk through with the enquirer in a supportive and encouraging way why the task was unachievable and to seek another way forward:

Let's try again – the first step is often the hardest – and remember the goal we are both aiming for is to put you back into the driving seat again – we both know you are capable of being there, but let's take it one step at a time.

The importance of evaluation

Monitoring and evaluation have become far more centre stage in recent years. There are several reasons for this. First, in some professions there have been a series of tragedies that have stunned the general public, causing high-level official inquiries to be established. As a result, more detailed guidance and practice guidelines have been set up in the hope that such tragedies never happen again. Monitoring and evaluation processes form part of that process. This, in turn, is part of the wider emphasis on evidence-based practice to ensure that practitioners use, and learn from, the available research and evaluation evidence.

Second, many helping organizations are now much more driven by a 'management by objectives' approach as the basis of what has come to be known as 'outcome-focused practice' (that is, practice where the desired outcomes are clear and explicit). In some cases, this is to ensure that the public money is properly spent and accounted for; in other cases, it is part of a drive to achieve greater levels of funding support for the work being undertaken. But, in all cases, it should be about making sure that what we set out to achieve together is actually achieved. In this climate, monitoring and evaluation play central roles.

A third reason is the one we wish to focus on here, not to underestimate the importance of the first two, but to locate the reason for monitoring and evaluation where we suggest it principally should lie: namely, in the commitment to best practice that is at the heart of the value base of the people work we undertake. If what we have been discussing in these chapters is as crucial as we have claimed – that the people we serve should be put centre stage of everything we do – then both they and we are entitled to know whether what we are offering is of any use whatsoever. How do we know that the help we have provided has been effective?

Key point

What right do we have to intervene in people's lives if we are not making a positive difference? It is therefore essential that we are able to be clear about whether our involvement is proving effective or not.

In our various professional groupings, we will doubtless have our monitoring and evaluation processes that will encourage us to reflect on what we have done and come to a judgement about its effectiveness. We will also be encouraged in professional supervision to reflect on these themes. In our own professional development, including the courses we attend, we will be increasingly aware of the contribution that evidence-based practice is making to our professional work, and how research findings can both inform and underpin the approaches we take in our work with others.

There is one further aspect, however, that in many ways should come top of the list. If our commitment is to a value base that puts the people we serve central to our work in all the ways we have so far been discussing, then it follows that we should be seeking the views of clients and carers to assess how effective our work together has been. In social work training, for example, students are now required to gain evidence from people who use their services and also from carers on how the student has worked with them, and how their work or approach might be improved.

There are admittedly some difficulties inherent in this approach. It is not always easy to gain honest and open feedback; sometimes people hold grudges and find it easier to complain than give balanced feedback. But this should not prevent individual workers and their organizations from seeking views about the help they have received and how it might be improved. This remains a central challenge that is inherent in our value base, and we ignore it at our peril.

Conclusion

Our focus in this chapter has been on person-centred care or, to put it another way, putting the people we serve at the centre of what we do. It involves making sure that we do not allow ourselves to be distracted by other pressures or to lose our focus on who and what is important.

As part of this, we have argued that effective monitoring and evaluation of our work is part of our commitment to best practice and thereby helps us make a difference to people's lives. It is to this theme of making a difference that we need to turn next.

Exercise 13

How can you evaluate your work? What steps can you take to make sure that what you are doing (or have done) is effective in achieving the agreed outcomes that should be guiding your practice?

Making a difference

Introduction

The concept of making a difference has underpinned much of our discussion so far, but it does deserve further, more detailed attention, such is its importance. It is a fundamental tenet of people work that the quality of service offered should be of the highest quality. The value base of people work helps us to understand that best practice should not be negotiable. This is not just because it is a matter of personal and professional pride that we, as professional people workers, should always do our best to deliver the best results. It is, rather, that our understanding of what it means to be human drives us inevitably to the conclusion that the essential dignity and worth of every individual demand that we do our best to be of service.

Achieving the highest standards

It would be naïve to pretend that this is an easy goal to achieve. Exactly the opposite is true. For all its lofty idealism, this ambition is often beyond our reach. As with parenting, so with our people work: we often have to make do with what is 'good enough'. This concept of 'good enough' helpfully reminds us that we all have to deal with pressures, tensions and challenges as parents, and that just to be able to bring our children up successfully against this, at times, chaotic back-drop is a triumph. Making a difference is easier said than done. There is, in fact, a real tension between the real and the ideal; between our aspirations and our achievements; between the goal of best practice and the level of service we often deliver. We must not allow the concept of perfection to prevent us from doing our best!

DOI: 10.4324/9781003689614-15

Even to hint at this, however, is to run the risk of serious rebuke, let alone misunderstanding. Surely, the critics will be hasty to proclaim: this is giving tacit approval of shoddy standards of care; surely there have been enough blunders by workers to warn us against the dangers of such an approach; surely people deserve better?

To this response the answers are no, yes and yes. It is not giving any sort of approval to shoddy standards; too many vulnerable people have been placed at far too great a risk to think for a moment that such an approach has merit; because yes, people do deserve better, much better. The value base of people work, and the main thrust of this entire manual, has been about best practice and the value base that underpins it.

Exploring our vulnerability

So, what is the issue being raised here? In essence, we are seeking to remind ourselves of our vulnerability and our flawed nature as human beings. There is a temptation to set up professional people workers, especially those who work and serve as leaders in faith communities, as role models of idealized human behaviour. Ordinary people may make a mess of their lives, but somehow we expect our professional workers to be above that sort of frailty. The media frenzy over politicians' sexual misdemeanours captures thispoint acutely: people in the public eye are expected to have a standard of morality that is often not expected of the 'ordinary person' who does not live in the public eye. And when they 'fall' (for all its theological overtones, this word is still used in popular parlance to capture the notion that the ideal has not been realized), then they should expect the full force of tabloid righteous indigna-tion to cascade around their ears – and so it does.

But, to be human is to be vulnerable, whether you are a politician or househusband, professional people worker or unemployed teenager, parent, spouse or friend. Professional training does not give people a protective armoury against the 'slings and arrows' of life's vicissitudes. Sometimes, it is the pressures generated by the very nature of people work that makes professional workers more, not less, vulnerable to problematic lifestyles and fractured relationships.

Ironically it can be the very striving for perfection that can be our worst enemy. We stay late at the office, having arrived early; we toil over our case files; we go more than the extra mile in doing our best for those we seek to help; we avidly peruse the latest research findings and consult journals to discover the latest the-oretical perspective to inform our practice. And still the demands from people increase daily – caseloads become overloaded; we can never do enough; and finally, we succumb to the stress and fall prey to what is often called 'burnout'. We have ceased to be any use to ourselves, and therefore of no use to others.

Papadatou (2009) proposes the notion of being 'vulnerable enough', by which she means managing the balance between allowing our fragility to overwhelm us, on the one hand, and adopting a hard protective skin that renders us insensitive.

Self-care is an essential part of our skills repertoire. Caring professionals are particularly prone to burnout because we have a tendency to put other people's needs before our own, sometimes to a dangerous extent.

In this chapter we explore the importance of personal development and learning in more detail, but at this point we are seeking to come to an honest appraisal of what can get in the way of delivering the best quality, evidence-based, values-based interventions. It is often the very qualities that make us such good people workers that become our Achilles' heel: the caring, compassionate approach to other people; the drive to give something back to the community; the passion for social justice; the desire to see a more fulfilled, fulfilling society for people to enjoy, where they can begin to thrive and reach their full potential. Without these attributes – and many more – our journey into people work would never have begun. But once we are on the journey, the risks both to our own self-fulfilment, and our capacity to move outside our own needs to begin to work creatively and effectively with others come crowding in.

Perhaps too we are often beset with the need for approval and to be liked, not just by our colleagues, but also by those we seek to help and support. Well, not by everyone perhaps – there will always be those difficult situations where we can't possibly hope to be liked, when we are taking actions that are bound to cause dismay and upset – but, if the majority can appreciate us and like us, then the warm glow inside us is replenished and we feel good about ourselves.

The risk in all of this, of course, is that, to use the title of this chapter, making a difference – it is often more our concern to make a difference to ourselves, rather than to the people we serve that is uppermost. How will this affect me? How will I come out of it? Do I need to cover my back? Or, at an even deeper level, how can I ensure that my own deep psychological and emotional needs will be satisfied, or my emotionally damaged spirit be protected? How far will my fears get the better of me?

This level of honesty and self-awareness does not come easily to us. In the 1960s, when encounter groups were popular, people who were training for a variety of helping professions were actively encouraged to explore their emotional lives in the context of group discussion and self-revelation. There was a belief that this approach would go a long way to ensure that emotional intelligence would be achieved by people, thereby enabling them to be more effective in their caring for others (that approach has now gone out of vogue, and may in some ways have driven some participants more into themselves in a turbulent introspection than into a more outward-facing approach to others). But, the need for self-awareness remains critical in all people work if we are to become part of a solution for other people, even if contemporary training programmes eschew the 1960s self-analysing approach (for a discussion of the concept of 'emotional intelligence', see Goleman, 1996, and, for a text with a specific focus on emotionally intelligent social work, see Howe, 2008).

> **Key point**
>
> Although the encounter group approach has largely been disregarded as being too extreme, the need for self-awareness and what is often referred to as 'use of self' remains very strong.

There may be an anomaly here. With the current emphasis upon evidence-based practice, people workers are constantly asking themselves the questions: What works? What research evidence is there to support this style of intervention? How will I know that my intervention has been effective? And, alongside these vitally important and relevant concerns, there is the need for self-awareness in the worker to ensure that they do not get superimposed upon the helping relationship. Far from being measurable, such concerns are much more intangible, for who among us is ever completely sure that our self-awareness is so comprehensive that we understand every twist and nuance that our own needs create within us? At best, we catch a glimpse of them from time to time, but, as for measuring them, then that is well beyond us. It will only be if our own deep psychological needs become disempowering to us, and cause us to need psychological intervention, that we may gain a fuller picture. Most of us, however, have to take responsibility for our professional practice by ensuring that we work within agency values and practice guidelines; that we use supervision honestly and effectively; that we record our interventions openly and in relevant detail; and most importantly, remember our human vulnerability and frailty that will mean that, from time to time, we will get it wrong. In that sense, we must never forget that the individual worker is never greater than the organization or agency they work for.

Spiritual intelligence: SQ

It is at this point, however, where the concept of spiritual intelligence (SQ) may have some useful things to say to us, building upon Goleman's (1996) work on emotional intelligence. The work of Zohar and Marshall (1999; 2004) encourages us to see a spiritual dimension in ourselves and in others, and to take account of this in our dealings with each other. Immediately, of course, there will come the query about what exactly this term 'spirituality' means, and what it has to do with the concepts we are discussing here. Some people have been misled by this term because they associate spirituality with religion. Spirituality is about finding meaning (which is why it is so often associated with belief systems like religion) but should not be equated with religion. The basic idea behind spiritual intelligence is that people need to find meaning in their work if they are to remain motivated and committed.

If we translate this into the context of people work, we can begin to explore the importance of spiritual intelligence by relating to some of the core indicators suggested by Zohar and Marshall. These include:

- the capacity to be flexible;
- a high degree of self-awareness;
- a capacity to face and use suffering;
- a capacity to face and transcend pain; and
- the quality of being inspired by vision and values.

These indicators bring us firmly back into the context of the values that inform our practice; they have a particular resonance with the theme of making a difference that we are currently exploring. In this case, though, the difference concerns ourselves as workers. It is about our motivation; our commitment; the impact our work has upon us as people, and the impact of us as people upon the work we undertake:

> It is our spiritual intelligence ... [Zohar and Marshall] argue which gives us an ultimate security upon which we can base our capacity to be innovative and creative. It is the SQ in so many people which drives their need for a sense of meaning and shared vision and purpose in the workplace, as well as in other areas of their lives.
>
> (Moss, 2004, p. 39)

Zohar and Marshall are suggesting, therefore, that this concept can be applied helpfully to how we understand and shape the culture of the organizations we work in. SQ therefore encourages us to explore ourselves and our attitudes to our work, and, most importantly, the value base that underpins our professional practice.

As we have already noted, we are not giving a narrow interpretation to the term 'spiritual' as if to suggest that it can only be used in association with belonging to a faith community or holding a set of specifically religious beliefs. Spirituality does indeed encompass these dimensions, but it is much wider than that. The term puts us in touch with whatever we mean by the 'essential humanity' deeply within us – what it means to be human; to be alive, rather than just existing. It raises profound issues of meaning and purpose that are at the heart of what it means to be human, irrespective of whether we also align ourselves with a particularly religious framework of understanding ourselves and the world.

But, by definition, the concept of the spiritual is not easy, perhaps even impossible, to measure. In a similar way to other great themes of being human – such as loving; sharing compassion; feeling passion; being overwhelmed by guilt or shame – we know intuitively that these are woven into the tapestry of our living, but the measurement of them is far too complex. But, these facets of being human lead to certain actions, and often our people work involves reaching out to people whose lives, for good or ill, are particularly strongly influenced by these emotions. As human beings we get things wrong, no matter who we are. Our spiritual intelligence, therefore, is saying something to us about alerting ourselves to these deeper aspects of being human and recognizing that we are more than just human 'doings' (Moss, 2002, p. 40). It alerts us to the need to recognize and value that essential humanity in each and every person and to ensure that our professional practice does not end up in some sort of scientific reductionism that denies the essential humanity of those we work with.

Gilbert (2010, p. 164) sums this up when he says about social work, but it can apply equally well to all people work, that it is:

> about recognising the individuality and innate dignity of each person, connecting with them, seeing the whole person in the context of their past and future aspirations, their family and neighbourhood, their community and connections. It is about building on integrity and creating trust and meaning, listening to and walking with, comprehending culture, race and creed, and engaging with the lived experience.

This reminds us once again of the essential value base of all people work, by pointing us not to essential differences between ourselves and those we serve, but to the essential shared humanity that we all have, with all its potential for success and failure, joy and pain, achievements and guilt, and meaning making. It is by recognizing this in ourselves and in others – this essential spirituality if you like – that opens up for us the possibility of effective relationships in working with others.

Again, Gilbert (2010, p. 75) captures this well when he comments that:

> the tragedies where human beings are cruel to other human beings occur when we fail to recognise the shared humanity in the person facing us. That distancing, of course, come so often from humankind's innate sense of separateness, disease and anxiety, leading to a need to distance ourselves and see ourselves as superior.

This takes us back to our previous discussion about the dangers of feeling that, as professional workers, we know best, and that we can use the power and influence that come with our professional roles in inappropriate ways that do not adequately reflect the value base of partnership working.

Conclusion

Whichever branch of the people professions you operate in, a key part of what your work will be all about is making a positive difference – generally with people who are ill, grieving, traumatized, dispossessed, discriminated against, excluded, alienated and/or facing various other challenges to their dignity, self-esteem and well-being. As we have seen, if we are to be both effective and ethical in helping people meet these challenges, we need to keep a firm grip on our values. We also need to take our own self-care needs seriously and to make sure that we do not lose sight of the importance of spirituality and essential humanity in everybody's life, not just those who are members of a faith community.

This discussion of what we mean by our essential humanity also opens up a further dimension of risk taking, that it may be argued is another essential (perhaps spiritual) capacity and value of being human. It is to this next important theme that we now turn in Chapter 15.

Exercise 14

How tuned in are you to your own self-care needs? What can you do to make sure that your passion for helping others does not place you at risk?

Promoting safety and positive risk taking

Introduction

There are, of course, risks involved in the work we do in the people professions: risks to the people we are seeking to support and empower that require us to adopt a protective role (safeguarding); risks that people are prepared to take to retain their dignity, wellbeing and identity; risks that what we are trying to do to help may backfire and do harm; and, sometimes, risks to ourselves. All of this makes for complex and demanding professional territory. It also makes for an area where once again values have a highly significant role to play.

As a way of grounding this discussion in the realities of practice, we begin with some real-life examples of the issues about promoting safety and positive risk taking. Once again, as you read through them, think carefully about the values issues they are raising.

Some living examples

1. When I was working in a psychiatric hospital on a long-stay acute ward, the consultant psychiatrist expressed a determination to break the mould of keeping the patients always cooped up in the ward. He arranged therefore for 20 of them to go to the local fair in the nearby town, accompanied by the right number of staff. Nineteen of them had a fantastic time and returned to the ward 'on a high' having had the best day of their lives for as long as they could remember. The one remaining patient went missing in the crowd and could not be traced for hours. Eventually the police found him – he had

DOI: 10.4324/9781003689614-16

wandered off to the nearby canal, had slipped in due to the previous heavy rainfall and drowned.

2. Melody was a young, newly qualified social worker who was sent to Mrs Davies, a 90-year-old woman living by herself in her own house where she had been for the past 40 years. Her husband had died ten years ago, and since then Mrs Davies's eyesight had been deteriorating steadily to the point where she had hardly any vision at all. Melody felt, when she visited, that Mrs Davies was becoming far too great a risk to be allowed to stay in her own home now that her sight had gone. She therefore tried to persuade her to move into sheltered accommodation and began to make arrangements for her to visit a local home. Mrs Davies fiercely resisted this proposal, claiming that it was an insult to her and would take away her independence.

3. Yousif worked with a group of young teenagers excluded from school because of their disruptive behaviour. He felt that it would be a valuable learning experience to take them on a trip to the Lake District for an adventure holiday, involving canoeing; orienteering; rock climbing; and pony trekking. He was conscious that, among the group of 12 young people, three had offences of burglary and theft, and he was not at all sure that they would be able to resist the opportunities presented by their week's stay in Keswick. He was also aware that two male members of the group had close relationships with two female group members who saw the adventure week more in terms of sexual activity than the programme that Yousif and his team had put together.

4. Fernando (aged 24) had been unemployed for two years, and during that time had accumulated large debts that had eventually driven him to seek advice from his local CAB. Over a period of 12 months, he managed with their help to reduce the debt considerably. One day he came to see his debt adviser with the news that he had been given the opportunity to buy a window cleaning round from a friend of his father who had had a heart attack and had had to give up work. The cost of the business, including the van and all equipment, would involve Fernando going heavily into debt once more.

5. Carla had been discharged from hospital into a local hostel, having experienced serious mental health problems. She was told very clearly by her psychiatrist that she must take her daily medication without fail if she wanted to stay well. At first, she enjoyed the life in the hostel, but after a few months found it claustrophobic and asked if she could move out into one of the halfway flats that had become available. The staff agreed and she moved in. She began to feel so much better and found part-time secretarial work. She decided that she no longer needed to take her medication. Dawn, her support worker, began to realize that Carla was beginning to slip back from the progress she had been making, but every time she asked about the medication, Carla said she was taking it and told Dawn to stop nagging.

6. Fred was the chair of the local residents' association on a small estate that had a wide cross-section of the community, including a primary school that brought children in from a wide catchment area, and offered playgroup and

after-school activities. The local probation office also had a number of 'safe houses' in the area, two of which were on Fred's estate. Fred knew that most of the men in these safe houses probably posed little threat to the community, but when he read in the local press that a well-known local sex offender had been granted parole and was likely to be given accommodation in one of the safe houses, he was irate. He went to see Johann, the senior probation officer, and demanded to know the full story, and for the name of the man on the sex offenders register to be widely publicized in order to protect the young people and children who attended the local school.

These cameos, appropriately anonymized, have all been real examples that illustrate some of the practical dilemmas facing people workers who are trying to balance several key considerations. These include:

- the individual's right to privacy;
- public safety;
- the individual's right, and sometimes need, to take risks;
- the impact of such risk taking on others.

It is no surprise, therefore, that risk assessment is now so often such a core, fundamental part of the professional people worker's role and responsibility.

Problems with defining risk

However, it is perhaps ironic that it is difficult to come up with a clear definition of what is meant by risk. Risk is sometimes used synonymously with danger, but this is not always helpful. In our daily lives, each and every one of us takes risks and is involved in calculating the likely effect – from the mundane crossing the road to making an investment; buying a lottery ticket; taking out a loan; entering a new relationship or going rock climbing and other 'high-risk' sports. 'Playing it safe' may be regarded by some as a virtue, but for many people 'risk taking' is an essential element of what it means to be human, a key part of their identity. There may only be a tiny minority who take this to ultimate extremes like sailing 'solo' round the world, but for most people a life without some frisson of risk, challenge and excitement would be a 'non-life' – existing, not living.

The dilemmas facing workers, as illustrated by the case examples that introduced this chapter, concern the assessment of when a risk turns into a danger, either to the individual or to others, and in those instances where the burden of responsibility should lie. Pierson and Thomas (2002, p. 413) capture this well when they observe that:

A child 'at risk' is regarded as vulnerable to physical or sexual abuse by one or more people, or to other sources of harm through parental neglect. What is rarely stated is the probability that the child will suffer some harm. This is the drawback of the phrase; it is used widely but with little agreement over the actual chance that a client deemed at risk will come to some harm. Care professionals also use the word in the sense of 'risk-taking', which means making a conscious decision to put something at stake in order to make possible a worthwhile gain or benefit.

There is not scope in this chapter to discuss all the intricacies of risk taking and risk assessment in the practice experience of the range of human services being covered in this manual. But, one crucial aspect is the direct link to the value base of our work. There is a danger that professional workers will tend to 'play it safe' when exploring options with those who use their services. They will err on the side of caution, not least because of the accountability they have for their actions and decisions, and the fear that, if something 'backfires', they will be held to account.

It is here that the judgement between risk and danger becomes of paramount importance: a child, or an older person, at risk of abuse lays upon the worker an obligation to ensure that safety and protection are made available. But, there is another line to be drawn: the line that respects an individual's wish, or need, to take risks in order to feel that they are still (to use the popular phrase) 'alive and kicking', and have a useful contribution to make to society. We noted earlier the importance of identity, and so trying to take away the risks that make us who we are is therefore highly problematic.

Reflective moment

What risks do you take that you feel are part of you are (driving, parenting, engaging in sports)? What effect would it have on you if someone were to deny you the right to take such risks 'for your own good'?

The value base relating to respecting and valuing people as individuals needs to include this 'risk-taking' element, so that people can lead as full, enriched and empowered lives as possible, within whatever limitations may have been imposed by health or circumstances (including court orders, of course). This can pose a particular set of challenges, as Davis (1996) argues:

> Risk taking ... is an essential element of working with mental health service users to ensure autonomy, choice and social participation. It is a means of challenging the paternalism and *overprotectiveness* of mental health services.

> (p. 114, emphasis added)

Working with older people provides further examples. Sue Thompson (2005, p. 39) reflects on situations where:

> older people are conceptualized en masse as frail and confused, it is all too often seen as one's duty [as a worker] to ensure that they are protected from risk, such as living in houses that are in poor repair, or not following guidelines on healthy eating. While this desire to protect is, in many ways, an admirable one, it has to be balanced with a respect for rights if it is not to be oppressive.

She goes on to argue that:

> while others may not agree with the choices we make, we expect them to respect our right to do so, as it indicates respect for our competence in making judgements. When a paternalistic approach is applied across the board, purely on age grounds, it assumes a lack of competence across the board. Listening to individuals can help to challenge this by highlighting difference.
>
> (pp. 39–40)

Here again we come back to the issue of power and the temptation experienced by professional workers to feel that they know best. Overprotectiveness is a synonym for 'playing it safe' from the worker's perspective, but a constant challenge arising from our professional value base is the extent to which we recognize and respect this dimension of individual worth, by celebrating and encouraging people to take risks as a fundamental expression of their humanity.

Conclusion

Risk taking is part of everyday life. It therefore needs to be *managed*, rather than *avoided*, as a 'risk-averse' approach has the potential to be oppressive by denying people rights and choice. We therefore need to make sure that the pressures involved in managing risk do not lead us to abandon our values and become over-protective and intrusive.

Exercise 15

We can often find ourselves under pressure from family members, other professionals and/or managers to act in risk-averse ways (that is to become over-protective and seek to deny people the right to take risks). What steps can we take to manage such situations without losing sight of our values?

Values today and tomorrow

Introduction

There is a long tradition of reflecting on values dating back to at least the Ancient Greek philosophers. But, where are we up to today in the modern world as far as values are concerned and what direction do we seem to be heading in? These questions are what this final chapter are about. Our aims are threefold. First, we are re-emphasizing the need to see values as part of a broader sociological picture and not simply a matter of personal ethics. Second, we are highlighting how values are part of a constantly changing and evolving landscape: much changes, but much also stays the same (the importance of being values driven, for example). Finally, our aim is to give you plenty of food for thought by presenting a range of interesting and important ideas that, in our view, merit careful consideration.

The work of Haidt (2014) encapsulates all three aims. He shows how a sense of morality (and thus values) varies from society to society and over time. In particular, he examines the differences between individualistic societies (broadly western) and sociocentric societies (mainly eastern) that focus more on collective concerns than individual ones. He describes an experiment that shows differences in terms of what is regarded as acceptable or unacceptable behaviour and attitudes. So, we should be ready to recognize that, however much commonality there might be about values, they are not set in stone. This leads us to ask: How have values changed and how are they likely to change? Such changes will, of course, affect not only society in general, but also professional practice.

The changing world of work

In Chapter 9, we noted the significant ways in which the world of work has been changing (and is likely to continue changing). The growing role and influence of artificial intelligence (AI) is predicted to make drastic changes in working life. This raises a number of questions, both general and specific. In general terms, AI will make many current manual work processes redundant and may even force a rethink of the world of work in terms of the 'work ethic'. Moral judgements are commonly made of people who choose not to be gainfully employed (unless, of course, they are independently wealthy). But if, as widely predicted, AI significantly reduces employment opportunities, should those who choose to fill their lives with other meaningful and fulfilling activities continue to be stigmatized?

The concept of 'universal basic income' (UBI) has attracted considerable interest in some quarters (see, for example, Bregman, 2016). It is based on the idea that, if governments provide a basic level of income for all citizens, this can largely eradicate poverty and related social problems. The argument is that the payments could be funded by savings in welfare benefits and their complex and costly administration, savings to the health service (given the close links between poverty and ill-health, including mental health) and government spending on a wide range of poverty-related social problems. This would give opportunities for those who want to work to do so, but those who do not wish to would not need to. The income level would be, as the name implies, basic, and so there would be considerable motivation to achieve higher levels of income through employment if desired. There are various arguments for and against UBI, but the changing world of work is likely to increase the level of interest in it. The value judgements around the role of work in people's lives are therefore likely to be reviewed.

The growing use of AI is also likely to have other implications in terms of values, not least the following.

Plagiarism

AI engines can be used to write essays, whether as college or university assignments or for publication in a journalistic or literary context. The facility to produce written work without writing it yourself and presenting it as if you had is now freely available. Of course, this raises questions of honesty and integrity. Given the ease with which such written work can be produced, we are left wondering how many otherwise ethical people will be tempted to take this option. It is not difficult to imagine a situation where an overloaded but values-driven student makes the mistake of using AI to *write* an essay (that is, not simply to research the essay, which is quite legitimate). The university's plagiarism detectors identify that it is not the student's original work, and so the student now faces potentially career-wrecking disciplinary proceedings and possibly removal from their course. The stakes in using AI to cheat are therefore very high.

Sexism

AI relies on a set of algorithms, automated processes of information management. Criado Perez (2019) provides a number of examples of how AI, if not programmed with equality in mind, can produce biased processes that are detrimental to the interests of women. That is, if steps are not taken to prevent it, the results can be profoundly sexist. As Criado Perez puts it:

> there are substantial gaps in government thinking and the result is that governments produce male-biased policy that is harming women. These data gaps are a result of failing to collect data, but they are also in part as a result of the male dominance of governments around the world.
>
> (p. 265)

In the computing world, the GIGO principle is well established: Garbage In, Garbage Out which basically means that input errors will produce output errors. Perhaps we can characterize the current situation in terms of the DIDO principle: Discrimination In, Discrimination Out.

Racism

Similar concerns have been raised about racism. We are becoming increasingly aware of the way computer programmes make decisions that can have a big impact on racial equality. This is especially important because the algorithms are being used more and more in areas like healthcare, the justice system and employment. It has been discovered that these algorithms can actually make existing racial biases worse. As with the sexism example above, one problem is the information they are trained on. If that information reflects existing patterns of racial or ethnic bias, the algorithm will just repeat those patterns.

Another issue is that, even if you do not specifically tell an algorithm to consider race, it can still figure it out indirectly. For example, if an algorithm is used to predict who might commit a crime and it is trained on data that shows that more black people are arrested, it might unfairly target black communities, even if it is not directly programmed to look at race. This is known as 'proxy discrimination' (Kassam and Marino, 2022).

What should be clear from this is that it is essential that the use of algorithms as part of AI usage is rooted in anti-discriminatory values. This presents significant challenges when we consider how rapid and widespread the massive growth of AI usage has become.

Neoliberalism and beyond

Neoliberalism is a political and economic ideology that has been dominant across much of the world for several decades. Its main premise is that the market should be given free rein to find its own level, as it is assumed within this mode of thinking that this will produce the best results. It is based on the principle of 'trickle-down economics', the idea that, as more wealth is generated, the benefits trickle down to the lower levels of economic status – that is, as the rich get richer, the poor and people at large also benefit. As Monbiot and Hutchison (2024) and various others point out, this principle bears no resemblance to reality which, instead, is characterized by growing inequality (defined as the gap between the richest and the poorest). It has produced political and economic systems that seek to reduce the regulatory role of the state to the bare minimum, leading to extensive privatization of public services, with citizens losing control of many aspects of services they may rely on.

From a values perspective, Dorling (2015) has argued convincingly that neoliberalism is characterized by an acceptance of greed as a legitimate value position. The emphasis on consumerist values that the pursuit of wealth engenders serves as an obstacle to more progressive social values. As we shall note below, it has also contributed to a sense of spiritual diminishment.

The financial crash of 2008 was, in large part, brought about by a lack of regulation of high-risk loans, a direct result of neoliberalism. However, the wider sociopolitical picture is not fixed or static. For example, Varoufakis (2024) argues that we have now moved to a new economic and political stage of development that he refers to as 'techno-feudalism'. The basic thrust of his argument is that the traditional concept of profit is now being replaced by a form of rent. The 'feudalism' element of the term derives from this emphasis on rent, just as the feudal lords took rent from their 'serfs' who were required to pay in kind (a percentage of the food they produced, for example) or in the form of labour undertaken for the lord. But now, Veroufakis argues, the rent is in a technological form, hence the 'techno' element of the term.

Rent, in its techno-feudalist sense, refers to the payments made in subscription form for access to cloud services such as television, video and music streaming and various other data-driven services. What makes this 'feudal' is that much of the data is gathered from the public – the equivalent of serfs providing labour for the lord of the manor.

Where this development takes us remains to be seen, but one thing seems certain: values shape and are shaped by what happens in the broader context. As society changes, it becomes all the more necessary to be clear about what our values are and what they need to be to adapt to the wider changes and to maintain our integrity within that context.

The future of democracy

For quite some time now there has been concern about a perceived shift to the political right across many parts of the world, with the potential for a re-emergence of fascism to be realized (Luce, 2018; Albright, 2018). This has led to concerns about threats to democracy as a result of an emboldening of authoritarianism (Levitsky and Ziblatt, 2018).

Added to this are emerging signs of a shift in the direction of oligarchy, by which we mean the concentration of power in a relatively small number of extremely wealthy people (oligarchy comes from the Greek for rule by the few). This takes us back to Varoufakis' concept of techno-feudalism, given the massive accumulation of great wealth by the 'tech giants' of Meta, Amazon, Google and so on. The example of Elon Musk, the owner of the X social media platform, taking up a senior role in Donald Trump's government in the United States adds a further dimension to this. Interestingly, Plato (in *The Republic*) warned that the concentration of wealth and power in the hands of the few could create a number of problems for how states are run.

The demise of the Soviet Union led to a major shift from a government-controlled economy to a free-market one more in keeping with the West. What this change facilitated was the creation of a class of extremely wealthy people who came to be known as oligarchs. The privatization of state-owned assets created opportunities for those people who were well placed to benefit from the changes to accumulate vast wealth. This involved gaining control of key industries, such as oil and gas, giving these oligarchs not only immense wealth, but also the opportunity to wield considerable power. The rise of techno-feudalism has now created parallel opportunities for major technology companies in the West.

One way of describing this situation is in terms of the Ancient Greek definition of democracy (the rule of the people by the people for the people) evolving, via neoliberalism, to the rule of the people by the rich for the rich to, via techno-feudalism, to the rule of the people by the super-rich for the super-rich). This reflects how the wealthy elite can use their resources to influence politicians and the law in ways that are in their favour and not necessarily of benefit to, or related to the needs and interests of, ordinary people. As with neoliberalism, the result is increasing inequality with all the problems this engenders. From a values perspective, this involves reinforcing greed and undermining equality, diversity, inclusion and compassion.

Once again, we have no way of knowing for certain where these developments will take us, but our concerns should help us to recognize the need to be clear about our values and how to use them to protect our personal and collective interests.

Religion and spirituality

The picture of the role of religion across the world is changing. According to the Pew Research Center (2015), if current trends continue, by 2050:

- The number of Muslims will nearly equal the number of Christians around the world.
- Atheists, agnostics and other people who do not affiliate with any religion – though increasing in countries such as the United States and France – will make up a declining share of the world's total population.

- The global Buddhist population will be about the same size it was in 2010, while the Hindu and Jewish populations will be larger than they are today.
- In Europe, Muslims will make up 10 per cent of the overall population.
- India will retain a Hindu majority but also will have the largest Muslim population of any country in the world, surpassing Indonesia.
- In the United States, Christians will decline from more than three-quarters of the population in 2010 to two-thirds in 2050, and Judaism will no longer be the largest non-Christian religion. Muslims will be more numerous in the U.S. than people who identify as Jewish on the basis of religion.
- Four out of every ten Christians in the world will live in sub-Saharan Africa.

Given the significance of religion as a basis for values, this picture of 'shifting sands' raises some interesting issues in terms of how values (and potential conflicts of values) will shape different societies, cultures and communities.

The growth of Islam and its influence are particularly significant, given the dual problems of Islamophobia and Islamist terrorism. Warsi (2024) provides a long list of examples of Islamophobia – that is, incidences of discrimination against Muslims, alerting us to the need for values-based practice to be attuned to such matters. What has complicated the situation is that the 9/11 attacks and other incidences associated with Islamist terror groups have generated considerable anti-Muslim sentiment in many quarters, even though it is vitally important to distinguish between Islam as a religion of peace and a minority of Muslims who perpetrate terrorist acts. Indeed, the vast majority of Muslims do not support terrorist acts (Pew Research Center, 2017).

Also of significance is the numerical decline of Christianity in the UK and the USA. While it would be a mistake to assume that the relative decline of Christianity can be equated with a decline in moral values, there remains the question of how values may change or evolve as a result of a lower level of influence from the Christian church. The relative decline will partly be accounted for by the growth of Islam, but also by the development of what had come to be known as being 'spiritual but not religious' (Parsons, 2018) – that is, being committed to a sense of spirituality (including values) but without subscribing to any particular religious belief system.

Religious values are represented in formal tracts, although how they are interpreted can vary enormously in terms of both different sects emphasizing different aspects and individuals engaging with values through their own personal beliefs and experiences and the influence of their specific social and cultural circumstances. With non-religious spirituality, there is less emphasis on formal tracts, but that is not to say that value choices are left purely to the individual. Even in the absence of religious 'rules', there will still be strong formal or semi-formal influences on values through, for example, political affiliations, ethical principles (veganism, for example), cultural norms, professional expectations and so on. But, here again, there will be much scope for individual interpretations and, indeed, personal value choices based entirely on the individual's own experiences and choices. So, as the world of religion changes, the values land-scape also evolves.

Values and the media

In our earlier discussion of PCS analysis, we noted that values are not just personal (P), they also have cultural (C) and structural (S) dimensions. Part of the cultural element is the role of the media. People do not operate in a social vacuum – we are all influenced to a greater or lesser extent by the information and ideas presented to us.

The mass media play a key role in shaping public opinion, but they do not do so in a values-free way. Information gleaned from the media therefore needs to be considered critically. This is because the interests of media barons (see the dis-cussion of oligarchy above) do not necessarily coincide with the interests of the wider populace. The actual or potential basis of the media has been highlighted in recent years as a feature of the shift to the political right. A prime example of this is the notion of 'alternative facts' that has come to be associated with Donald Trump whose estrangement from the truth has been well documented.

Maintaining values-based practice therefore depends in part on being aware of misinformation and disinformation. The two terms are often used interchange-ably, but they are actually different. Misinformation includes inaccurate, biased or stereotypical information that can have problematic consequences – for example, when information is presented in a gender-biased way that affords women less authority and credibility than men (Sieghart, 2022). It reflects underlying cultural assumptions (C) that, in turn, reflect wider social structures (S). Disinformation is very similar and has parallel consequences in terms of bias and discrimination, but the key difference is that disinformation is *intentional,* it is a political strategy specifically designed to affect the views of either people in general or a particular group or category of people. An example would be Donald Trump claiming that President Zelensky's popularity rating was 4 per cent when in fact it was 57 per cent.

In terms of values-based practice, the lesson we can learn here is that, while information from the media cannot be discounted altogether, it needs to be handled critically. If we adopt information uncritically, we may be acting against our values without even realizing that we are doing so, misled by untrustworthy information.

Environmental challenges

While the Earth, our habitat, is robust and resilient in many ways, the evidence that we are destroying our environment is mounting, despite the resistance in some parts to accepting what the science clearly tells us. This presents humanity with a number of challenges, including challenges around values. For example, does the value of compassion apply to future generations or is it limited to those we know directly, the people who matter to us personally?

What is interesting in terms of climate change is the work of eminent sociologist Ulrich Beck who argues that environmental concerns introduce a new layer of inequality based on geography (Beck, 2016). As the impact of climate change brings about significant geographic changes (rising sea levels making some locations uninhabitable), there will be those whose lack of power and resources means they will lose out, as distinct from those who have the wealth and power to secure alternative safer living accommodation. So, in this regard, a new form of inequality will connect with existing inequalities to heighten the gaps between the haves and have-nots.

What is also interesting about Beck's approach is that he sees possible positive developments from this. He envisages the global nature of the crisis forcing governments and transnational organizations to work together constructively to address the problems, potentially breaking down existing obstacles to cooperation and mutual benefit. How realistic this is remains to be seen, but it certainly raises important questions about the role values will play in responding to such major challenges.

The wellbeing economy

Some time ago social policy expert Bill Jordan introduced the concept of a 'wellbeing economy' (Jordan, 2008). He argues that a healthy economy is not just about financial matters. It is – or should be – also about promoting quality of life and a strong society. He bemoans the emphasis on material wealth and the relative lack of attention paid to health, wellbeing, positive social relations and a sense of belonging.

He argues that the way the economy is currently managed actually makes things worse, as the emphasis on material factors stands in the way of people finding fulfilment in other ways. He proposes that there should be a stronger focus on making policies that help people feel good about their lives and their communities. This should include such factors as trust, participation in communities and relationships. Fundamentally, what he is saying is that, while he recognizes the need for an efficient and effective economy, financial matters are not the only things that matter. He is therefore proposing a significant value shift from an overemphasis on material factors to a more holistic approach that more fully incorporates quality of life. This is a good example of how values need to be understood not only in personal terms, but also much more broadly.

Conclusion

Societies are not static entities. They are constantly changing, sometimes in subtle, barely noticeable ways, sometimes in fairly drastic ways. For example, there has been much speculation about how the COVID-19 pandemic changed society, not least in terms of the shift towards remote and hybrid working. In particular, as we have noted, the political shift to the right has been quite pronounced, with significant implications for society in general and professional practice in particular that are quite discernible.

West (2025) makes the important point that: 'Our values are the blueprint for the world we'd like to live in. Our politics are the roadmap directing us to that world' (p. xi). So, if we want to have as full an understanding of values as we can, then we have to locate the subject in the broader field of the constantly changing and evolving sociopolitical context. We hope that the discussions in this chapter will have helped you to recognize this and to be prepared to engage with the complexities of the social and political context in which values-based practice necessarily operates.

Exercise 16
In terms of all the issues raised in this chapter, which do you think is the most significant for you and your circumstances? What implications does it give rise to?

CHAPTER 17

Conclusion

Throughout the manual we have been brought back time and time again to ourselves and our values and to the ways in which, whatever our individual 'take' may be on a specific issue, we can operationalize the professional value base of our agency in the work we do with the people we serve. Values are not like the welfare benefits system that provides us with an annual handbook of benefit rates that we can apply on a fairly mechanistic basis to a particular situation. Instead, they get under our skin and bite deep and affect who we are: as professional workers our principal 'tool' is ourselves, and our values deeply affect how we regard, treat and interact with people. Therefore, this manual should constantly challenge us and will act as a mirror in which we look carefully at our values-based practice. It challenges us to examine the extent to which we are part of a solution or part of the problem as far as the people we serve are concerned. It raises the issue of the extent to which we are anti-discriminatory in our approach.

The value base underpinning practice is an essential area of study for everyone involved in the people professions. We cannot hope to achieve good practice unless we appreciate the central role of values, particularly in terms of the various areas we have covered here in each of the different chapters that go to make up the manual.

These, then, are crucial aspects of good practice, and they all reflect what is perhaps the most fundamental value – that of valuing people, treating all people as important and therefore with respect and dignity. This manual can play a part in developing the skills and values we need to provide the best possible practice for supporting and empowering the people we work with. However, we should

DOI: 10.4324/9781003689614-18

not become complacent and assume that studying this manual is all that is needed. Indeed, this manual should be seen as the beginning of the process, rather than the end of it.

By definition, a manual such as this does not have a neat and tidy conclusion: that is for you, the reader, not the authors, to determine. We hope that, in the process of engaging with this manual and the issues that have been raised, you will have made considerable progress on this all-important journey. The pace of your progress has been yours to determine throughout.

Our hope is that you will have gained an even clearer picture of the central importance of values for everything you will do within your professional practice, and that this manual has already been a springboard for you to explore and wrestle with some of the exciting and crucial issues other authors have written about in depth.

Promoting values-based practice involves developing a range of skills. Skill development is a long-term process, and so your studies can only help you along the way – they cannot provide you with all the answers. The task, therefore, is to carry on learning, to use the knowledge gained not as an end in itself, but as steps towards future learning – part of a process of continuous professional development. So, congratulations on completing the manual. We hope you have found it useful and stimulating and well worth the hard work you have put into it. We also hope you will share our view of learning as a continuous process – one from which you will gain considerable benefit, enjoyment and pride.

Guide to further learning

Books and academic journals

Clarke, A. and Hughes, D. (2016) *Professional Decision-Making in Social Work: An Introduction*. London, Bloomsbury. This book offers insights into professional decision making within social work and discusses the importance of values in practice.

Gillon, R. (2015) *Values-Based Practice: A New Approach to Decision-Making in the Helping Professions*. Wiley-Blackwell. This foundational text outlines the theoretical underpinnings of values-based practice, providing an excellent introduction to how values influence decision making in the helping professions.

Hawksworth, W. (2016) *Applying Person-Centred Care in Mental Health: A Guide to Values-Based Practice*, Brighton, Pavilion

Holloway, M. and Moss, B. (2010) *Spirituality and Social Work*, Basingstoke, Palgrave Macmillan.

Thompson, N. (2017) *Social Problems and Social Justice*, London, Bloomsbury.

Thompson, N. (2018) *Promoting Equality: Working with Diversity and Difference*, 4th edn, London, Bloomsbury.

Thompson, N. (2021) *Anti-discriminatory Practice: Equality, Diversity and Social Justice*, 7th edn, London, Bloomsbury.

Ethics and Social Welfare Journal: This academic journal publishes cutting-edge research on ethics, including values-based practice, in the context of social welfare and the helping professions.

Research and reports

Department of Health (2018) *Values in Healthcare: A Values-Based Approach to Patient-Centered Care*. Department of Health. This government report offers insights into how values-based approaches can shape patient care, particularly in healthcare settings.

NHS England (2017) *Values-Based Recruitment: A Framework for Healthcare Professionals*. The NHS report offers a framework on how values-based recruitment can foster more effective healthcare teams by ensuring that personal values align with professional ethical standards.

Health Foundation (2020) *The Role of Values in Healthcare Practice*. This report from a UK charity discusses how understanding and integrating values into healthcare practice can lead to better patient outcomes and practitioner satisfaction.

Scottish Government (2017) *Person-Centred Health and Care: Values-Based Approach*. This report from Scotland's government highlights the importance of incorporating values into healthcare delivery and provides a model for embedding these principles into practice.

Online resources and websites

The British Association of Social Workers (BASW) (www.basw.co.uk)

BASW provides numerous resources related to values, ethics and practice in social work. Their website includes articles, webinars and access to professional development opportunities.

Centre for Policy on Ageing (www.cpa.org.uk)

Equality and Human Rights Commission www.equalityhumanrights.com

humansolutions (www.humansolutions.info)

The Ethical Professional Practice Network (www.eppn.org.uk)

An online platform dedicated to ethical practice and values in the helping professions. It offers resources on training, ethics discussions and tools to assist practitioners in ethical decision making.

Liberty (www.libertyhumanrights.org.uk)

National Autistic Society (www.autism.org.uk)

Stonewall (www.stonewall.org.uk)

The Values-Based Practice Network (www.valuesbasedpractice.org)

This online network provides a wide range of resources, including articles, case studies, and videos that explore the role of values in healthcare and the helping professions. The website also offers links to conferences and workshops on values-based practice.

Training resources

Centre for Values-Based Practice in Health and Social Care (www.valuesbasedpractice. org/centre)

This training centre offers workshops, webinars and resources designed to help professionals integrate values-based practice into their daily work. The centre also offers certification programmes for practitioners wishing to specialize in this field.

Hawksworth, W. (2016) *Applying Person-Centred Care in Mental Health: A Guide to Values-Based Practice*, Brighton, Pavilion.

Hawksworth, W. (2016) *ApplyingValues-basedPracticeforPeopleExperiencing Psychosis*,Brighton,Pavilion.

Murphy, B., Bradshaw, K. and Beadle-Brown J. (2017) *Person-centredActiveSupport Trai ningPack*,2ndedn,Brighton,Pavilion.

NHS Leadership Academy (www.leadershipacademy.nhs.uk)

The NHS Leadership Academy provides a range of leadership programs that integrate values-based practice with leadership development in healthcare settings.

Robinson, J. and Thompson, S. (2019) *Working with Adults: Values into Practice: A Learning and Development Manual*, 2nd edn, Brighton, Pavilion.

Thompson, N. (2019) *Promoting Equality, Valuing Diversity: A Learning and Development Manual*, 2nd edn, Brighton, Pavilion.

Thompson, N. and Moss, B. (2019) *Spirituality, Meaning and Values: A Learning and Development Manual,* 2nd edn, Brighton, Pavilion.

Key research articles and theories

Meleis, A. I.. and Clements, A. (2016) 'Values and Ethics in Nursing: A Practice-Based Approach'. *Journal of Nursing Care Quality*, 31(4), 279–86.

This article discusses how nurses can apply values and ethics in clinical practice, a key component of values-based practice in healthcare settings.

Mendelson, D. (2017) Ethical Decision-Making in Social Work: Understanding the Role of Values', *Journal of Social Work Values and Ethics*, 14(2), 15–24.

A deep dive into the role of values in social work decision making, with a focus on ethical dilemmas and conflict resolution.

Jorm, C. and Wright, L. (2015) 'Values-Based Practice in Mental Health: The Role of Personal Values in Clinical Decision-Making'. *Journal of Mental Health*, 24(5), 320–27.

This paper explores how mental health professionals can incorporate their personal values into decision making while respecting the values of their clients.

Professional organizations and associations

The World Health Organization (WHO) provides global perspectives on values-based practice, offering resources for practitioners worldwide on integrating values in healthcare settings.

The Royal College of Nursing (RCN) (www.rcn.org.uk)

The RCN offers a variety of publications and resources for nurses focusing on values-based care and the application of ethics in practice.

Social Care Institute for Excellence (SCIE) (www.scie.org.uk) offers online courses, practice guides, and publications that explore the role of values in social care and the ethical dilemmas faced by professionals in the sector.

References

Albright, M. (2018) *Fascism: A Warning*, London, William Collins.

Amos, V. and Ouseley, H. (1994) 'Foreword', in Cheung-Judge, M. and Henley, A. (1994) *Equality in Action*, London, NCVO.

Beck, U. (2016) *The Metamorphosis of the World*, Cambridge, Polity.

Bellis, M. A., Hughes, K., Ford, K., Ramos Rodriguez, G., Sethi, D. and Passmore, J. (2014) 'Life Course Health Consequences and Associated Annual Costs of Adverse Childhood Experiences across Europe and the United States', *The Lancet Public Health*, *373*(9657), pp. 68–78.

Bevan, S. and Cooper, C. L. (2022) *The Healthy Workforce: Enhancing Wellbeing and Productivity in the Workers of the Future*, Bingley, Emerald Publishing.

Biestek, F. (1961) *The Casework Relationship*, London, Allen and Unwin.

Blumstein, A. (2015) Racial Disproportionality in Prisons, in Bangs, R. and Davis, L. E. (eds) *Race and Social Problems*, New York, Springer.

Bregman, R. (2016) *Utopia for Realists: The Case for a Universal Basic Income, Open Borders, and a 15-hour Workweek*, Amsterdam, The Correspondent.

British Association of Social Workers (2014) *The Code of Ethics for Social Work*, Birmingham, BASW Publications.

Burnard, P. and Chapman, C. (1999) *Professional and Ethical Issues in Nursing*, 2nd edn, London, Balliere-Tindall.

Cheese, P. (2021) *The New World of Work: Shaping a Future that Helps People, Organizations and Our Societies to Thrive*, London, Kogan Page.

Cheung-Judge, M. and Henley, A. (1994) *Equality in Action*, London, NCVO.

Clark, C. (2000) *Social Work Ethics: Politics, Principles and Practice*, Basingstoke, Palgrave Macmillan.

Coyte, M. E., Gilbert, P. and Nicholls, V. (2008) *Spirituality, Values and Mental Health: Jewels for the Journey*, London, Jessica Kingsley Publishing.

REFERENCES

Criado Perez, C. (2019) *Invisible Women: Exposing Data Bias in a World Designed for Men*, London, Chatto & Windus.

Davis, M. (1996) '*Risk Work and Mental Health*', in Kemshall, H. and Pritchard, J. (eds) *Good Practice in Risk Assessment and Risk Management 1*, London, Jessica Kingsley Publishers.

Dorling, D. (2015) *Injustice: Why Social Inequality Still Persists*, Bristol, Policy Press.

Durkheim, E. (1938) *The Rules of Sociological Method*, Translated by Sarah A. Solovay and John Mueller, 8th edn, Chicago, University of Chicago Press, originally published 1895.

Etzioni, A. (1995) *The Spirit of Community: Rights, Responsibilities and the Communitarian Agenda*, London, Fontana.

Gallup (2024) *State of the Global Workforce*. www.gallup.com/workplace/349484/state-of-the-global-workplace.aspx

Gilbert, P. (2010) *Social Work and Mental Health: The Value of Everything*, 2nd edn, Lyme Regis, Russell House Publishing.

Goleman, D. (1996) *Emotional Intelligence: Why it can Matter More than IQ*, London, Bloomsbury.

Hastings, A. and Matthews, P. (2011) *"Sharp Elbows": Do the Middle Classes Have Advantages in Public Services Provision and, if so, How?*, Project Report, Glasgow, University of Glasgow.

Hodge, D. (2003) *Spiritual Assessment: Handbook for Helping Professionals*, Botsford, CT, North American Association of Christians in Social Work.

Holloway, M. and Moss, B. (2010) *Spirituality and Social Work*, Basingstoke, Palgrave Macmillan.

Howe, D. (2008) *The Emotionally Intelligent Social Worker*, Basingstoke, Palgrave Macmillan.

Jordan, B. (2008) *Welfare and Well-being: Social Value in Public Policy*, Bristol, Policy Press.

Jowett, M. and O'Loughlin, S. (2005) *Social Work with Children and Families*, Exeter, Learning Matters.

Kassam, A. and Marino, P. (2022) 'Algorithmic Racial Discrimination', *Feminist Philosophy Quarterly*, 8(3/4).

Kirk, S. A., Gomory, T. and Cohen, D. (2015) *Mad Science: Psychiatric Coercion, Diagnosis and Drugs*, London, Transaction Publishers.

Levitsky, S. and Ziblatt, D. (2018) *How Democracies Die: What History Reveals about Our Future*, London, Penguin.

Luce, E. (2018) *The Retreat of Western Liberalism*, London, Abacus.

Macpherson, W. (1999) *The Stephen Lawrence Inquiry Report*, London, HMSO.

May, V. M. (2015) *Pursuing Intersectionality: Unsettling Dominant Imaginaries*, London, Routledge.

Monbiot, G. and Hutchison, P. (2024) *The Invisible Doctrine: The Secret History of Neoliberalism (& How it Came to Control Your Life)*, London, Allen Lane.

Moss, B. (2002) 'Spirituality: A Personal View', in Thompson, N. (ed.) *Loss and Grief: A Guide for Human Services Practitioners*, Basingstoke, Palgrave Macmillan.

Moss, B. (2004) TGIM: Thank God it's Monday, *British Journal of Occupational Learning* 2(2), pp. 33–43.

Moss, B. (2005) *Religion and Spirituality*, Lyme Regis, Russell House Publishing.

Oliver, M. (2009) *Understanding Disability: From Theory to Practice*, 2nd edn, Basingstoke, Palgrave Macmillan.

Papadatou, D. (2009) *In the Face of Death: Professionals who Care for the Dying and the Bereaved: Coping Strategies for the Helping Professional*. New York, Springer.

Parker, J. (2004) *Effective Practice Learning in Social Work*, Exeter, Learning Matters.

Parsons, B. (2018) *Being Spiritual But Not Religious: Past, Present, Future(s)*, London, Routledge.

Pew Research Center (2015) *The Future of World Religions: Population Growth Projections*, 2010–2050, www.pewresearch.org/religion/2015/04/02/religious-projecti ons-2010-2050/.

Pew Research Center (2017) *Muslims and Islam: Key Findings in the U.S. and Around the World*, www.pewresearch.org/short-reads/2017/08/09/muslims-and-islam-key-findi ngs-in-the-u-s-and-around-the-world/.

Pierson, J. and Thomas, M. (2002) *Collins Dictionary of Social Work*, 2nd edn, Glasgow, HarperCollins.

Rogers, C. (1961) *Client-centred Therapy*, London, Constable.

Rutter, M. (1999) Resilience Concepts and Findings: Implications for Family Therapy, *Journal of Family Therapy* 21, pp. 119–44.

Ryan, J. S. and Burchell, M. J. (2023) *Make Work Healthy: Create a Sustainable Organization with High-performing Employees*, Hoboken, NJ, Wiley.

Schön, D. (1983) *The Reflective Practitioner*, London, Temple Smith.

Schön, D. (1987) *Educating the Reflective Practitioner*, San Francisco, Jossey-Bass.

Shardlow, S. (1998) 'Values, Ethics and Social Work', in Adams *et al.* (1998) *Social Work: Themes, Issues and Critical Debates*, London, Macmillan.

Sieghart, M. A. (2022) *The Authority Gap: Why Women are Still Taken Less Seriously than Men, and What We Can Do about It*, London, Penguin.

Smale, G., Tuson, G. with Biehal, N. and Marsh, P. (1993) *Empowerment, Assessment, Care Management and the Skilled Worker*, London, HMSO.

Thompson, N. (2016) *The Professional Social Worker: Meeting the Challenge*, 2nd edn, London, Bloomsbury.

Thompson, N. (2017) *Theorizing Practice*, 2nd edn, London, Bloomsbury.

Thompson, N. (2018a) *Promoting Equality: Working with Diversity and Difference*, 4th edn, London, Bloomsbury.

Thompson, N. (2018b) *Applied Sociology*, New York, Routledge.

Thompson, N. (2018c) *Effective Communication: A Guide to Theory and Practice*, 3rd edn, London, Bloomsbury.

Thompson, N. (2019) *Mental Health and Well-being: Alternatives to the Medical Model*, New York, Routledge.

Thompson, N. (2021) *Anti-discriminatory Practice: Equality, Diversity and Social Justice*, 7th edn, London, Bloomsbury.

Thompson, N. (2022) *The Managing People Practice Manual*, Wrexham, Avenue Media Solutions.

Thompson, N. (2023) *The Social Worker's Practice Manual*, 2nd edn, London, Jessica Kingsley Publishers.

Thompson, N. (2024a) *Understanding Social Work: Preparing for Practice*, 6th edn, London, Bloomsbury.

Thompson, N. (2024b) *Managing Stress*, 2nd edn, London, Routledge.

Thompson, N. (2025) *Authentic Leadership Revisited*, 2nd edn, Cheltenham, Edward Elgar.

Thompson, N. and Cox, G. R. (eds) (2020) *Promoting Resilience, Responding to Adversity, Vulnerability, and Loss*, New York, Routledge.

REFERENCES

Thompson, N. and Cox, G. R. (2025) *Age and Dignity: Anti-ageist Theory and Practice*, Cheltenham, Edward Elgar.

Thompson, S. (2005) *Age Discrimination*, Lyme Regis, Russell House Publishing.

Thompson, S. (2025) *The Care of Older People: A Values Perspective*, 2nd edn, London, Routledge.

Thompson, S. and Thompson, N. (2023) *The Critically Reflective Practitioner*, 3rd edn, London, Bloomsbury.

Varoufakis, Y. (2024) *Technofeudalism: What Killed Capitalism*, London, Vintage.

Walsh, M. and Thompson, N. (2019) *Childhood Trauma and Recovery: A Child-centred Approach to Healing Early Years Abuse*, Brighton, Pavilion.

Warsi, S. (2024) *Muslims Don't Matter*, London, The Bridge Street Press.

West, K. (2025) *The Science of Racism*, London, Picador.

Wilkinson, D., Shemmings, D. and Pascoe, C. (2019) *Child Abuse: An Evidence Base for Confident Practice*, 5th edn, London, Open University Press.

Winnicott, D. W. (1965) *The Maturational Process and the Facilitative Environment*, New York, International Universities Press.

Woodbridge, K. and Fulford, K. W. M. (2004) *Whose Values? A Workbook for Values-based Practice in Mental Health Care*, London, The Sainsbury Centre for Mental Health.

Zohar, D. and Marshall, I. (1999) *SQ: Connecting with Our Spiritual Intelligence*, London, Bloomsbury.

Zohar, D. and Marshall, I. (2004) *Spiritual Capital: Wealth We Can Live By*, London, Bloomsbury.

For Product Safety Concerns and Information please contact our EU
representative GPSR@taylorandfrancis.com
Taylor & Francis Verlag GmbH, Kaufingerstraße 24, 80331 München, Germany

www.ingramcontent.com/pod-product-compliance
Lightning Source LLC
Chambersburg PA
CBHW052009270326
41929CB00015B/2850